GOD'S JOY FRUIT

Walking Through the Fields of Grace and Mercy in Bloom

Compiled By Angela R. Edwards

Compiled by Angela R. Edwards

God's JOY Fruit:
Walking Through the Fields of Grace and Mercy in Bloom

Compiled By:
Angela R. Edwards

Foreword By:
Rev. Dr. Marilyn E. Porter

Contributions By:
**CaTina Jenkins
Cindy H. Reed
Clarence Jordan, Jr.
Keywana Wright
Laurie Benoit
Marlowe R. Scott
Marvell Gales
Nikki Denise
Reyna Goynes
Sathya Callender
Shanericka Jones
Tondra "Poetic Sense" Mosley
Tosha Dearbone**

Redemption's Story Publishing, LLC, Houston, TX (USA)

God's Joy Fruit

God's JOY Fruit:
Walking Through the Fields of Grace and Mercy in Bloom

Copyright © 2020
Angela R. Edwards

All Rights Reserved.
No portion of this publication may be reproduced, stored in an electronic system, or transmitted in any form or by any means (electronic, mechanical, photocopy, recording, or otherwise) without written permission from the publisher. Brief quotations may be used in literary reviews.

Print ISBN: 978-1-947445-85-7
Digital ISBN: 978-1-947445-86-4

Scripture references are taken from the King James Version (KJV), New International Version (NIV), and Amplified Bible (AMP). Used with permission via Zondervan. Public Domain.

For information and bulk ordering, contact:
Redemption's Story Publishing, LLC
Angela Edwards, CEO
P.O. Box 62287
Houston, TX 77205
RedeemedByHim@Redemptions-Story.com

Compiled by Angela R. Edwards

Dedication

To anyone who has *ever* felt lonely and downtrodden;

To those who choose to embrace JOY in spite of…

This book is for YOU!

Acknowledgments

First and foremost, always giving honor and glory to the **Holy Trinity:** God the Father, God the Son, and God the Holy Spirit. Without Him, the gifts and talents instilled in me would not have blossomed into all He has destined for them to be for HIS Kingdom.

As always, to my patient, loving, and supportive husband, **James Edwards:** I appreciate your sacrifice of "our time" as I work tirelessly to build and maintain a legacy for our family. I love you!

To my children, **Anequilla Foots and Gerald Savage, III:** You, my babies, bring me JOY! I am grateful for your patience as I parented my way with you — bumps, bruises, and all! I love you both!

To my *BIGGEST* supporter on this side of Heaven — my mother, **Marlowe R. Scott:** I cannot begin to put all that you are to me in this book, as that would require a project all in its own. In this space, however, I shower you with love and appreciation for being MY Mommy! I love you beyond mere words!

To my bestie and Foreword-writer, **Marilyn E. Porter:** Thank you for, well, everything (giggles)! Your spiritual guidance, shoulder to cry on, and 40+ years of friendship are priceless. Where would I be with you? I love and appreciate you, Murl!

Compiled by Angela R. Edwards

To the host of **Contributing Authors** of *God's Joy Fruit*: Thank you **ALL** for readily-agreeing to sow your "JOY" stories into others. Each story is amazing and sure to impact the lives of our readers. My constant prayer is that collectively, we change lives with the power of our words. To God be the glory! Amen and AMEN!

Lastly, I acknowledge my supporters via social media channels. Know that I see you and truly appreciate your consistency at every turn. As it is said, *"Let's ride this thing out until the wheels fall off!"* Blessings to you **ALL**!

Foreword

Rev. Dr. Marilyn E. Porter

Oh, how I love to sink my teeth into some **JOY** fruit! *Mmm Mmm GOOD!*

As humans, we tend to gravitate to things that bring us temporal moments of fleeting happiness. We love the outer smiles that are actually often masks of inner turmoil. We engage in activities that appease our flesh but often leaves us with a hole in our very souls. Those moments often elude the sweetness of **JOY's** taste because we seek to be pleasured through our natural senses. Try, instead, engaging in the wonderful world of communication with our Heavenly Father. Therein lies the center of all **JOY**!

Compiled by Angela R. Edwards

This particular subject is one that I fear the *average* human being cannot truly testify to. We often shoot the shot when we attempt to speak of JOY, but the shot lands at happiness—something that is based on what happens or does not happen as the source. I say: **JESUS** is the center of all **JOY**! Richard Smallwood will be forever remembered as the man who brought us the magnificent "The Center of My Joy." A portion of the lyrics state, *"All that's good and perfect comes from You [Jesus]…"* The **CENTER** of **JOY** is fullness in the revelation of who Jesus Christ is and how much He sacrificed for you. The revelation of your absolute importance to our Savior overshadows, outshines, and overpowers every and any vile and wicked action that could ever happen!

JOY remains at the death of a parent or child.

JOY remains as the repo man drives off with your car.

JOY remains as you watch your home be auctioned off on the courthouse steps.

JOY remains as you sign the divorce papers.

JOY shows up in the room where the chemo treatments are happening.

JOY pushes through amid the lies and the scandalizing of your name.

I like to think of **JOY** as a person—a companion of mine that walks with me, talks with me, and tells me I am its own!

God's Joy Fruit

You got it: **JESUS IS JOY!** Without His presence in your life, you are destined to only obtain mere happiness.

As you read through the pages of this book, I want you to embrace the person of **JOY**. Rest in **JOY**! Shout out **JOY**! Jump for **JOY**! While you do those things, watch the happiness you've been so desperately trying to achieve become futile amid the victorious tastes of **JOY!**

Compiled by Angela R. Edwards

Introduction

What more is there to say about **"JOY"** when coming off the heels of Rev. Dr. Marilyn E. Porter's Foreword?! *Wow!*

In this second installment in the "God's Fruit" book series, *God's Joy Fruit: Walking the Fields of Grace and Mercy in Bloom*, each author contributed a story that speaks of a time when **JOY** was the furthest from their mind. You will read about moments of tragedy…turned **JOY**; pain…turned **JOY**; self-hatred…turned **JOY**, and so much more. While the enemy of our soul—Satan—tried to hold his grip tightly and gain another for his kingdom, each author regained their strength and said, *"NOT TODAY, DUDE!"*

Be encouraged! You will see how calling on the name of Jesus and His war angels changed circumstance after circumstance for His glory!

Be nourished! You will read stories that will shock you to your core, and then you will celebrate when you see how our Heavenly Father **ALWAYS** remains undefeated!

OH, THE *JOY!!!*

Take a moment to applaud **YOURSELF** for all that you've been through, yet here you are today. You may not feel *JOYFUL* at this moment, but embrace the stories shared within. There is surely **at least** one that will resonate with your spirit-man/spirit-woman. Then, when you arrive at the end, you are encouraged to pen your own **JOY** story. You have it in you! It's there, waiting for you to give it a voice — to bring it to life!

Your words have **POWER!** Send them into the atmosphere! Get your **JOY** today! Give God His glory, honor, and praise for carrying you through to *THIS* day — and then testify! Someone needs your testimony. Deny them no longer!

Compiled by Angela R. Edwards

Theme Text

"Rejoice always, pray continually, give thanks in all circumstances; for this is God's will for you in Christ Jesus."

1 Thessalonians 5:16-18

Table of Contents

DEDICATION	VI
ACKNOWLEDGMENTS	VII
FOREWORD	IX
INTRODUCTION	XII
THEME TEXT	XIV
TONDRA "POETIC SENSE" MOSLEY	
God's Joy-Bearing Fruit – A Poem	2
ANGELA R. EDWARDS	
Seven, Seven, Seven Years	4
MARLOWE R. SCOTT	
Joy – My Found Answer	9
LAURIE BENOIT	
A Journey to Joy	17
REYNA HARRIS-GOYNES	
Life's Ultimate Joy	25
TOSHA R. DEARBONE	
Mirrors Don't Lie	33
CATINA JENKINS	
After the Pain	41
SATHYA CALLENDER	
The Joy I Felt When	48
KEYWANA WRIGHT	
Finding the Joy After the Pain	53
CINDY H. REED	
My Journey — God's Delivery	60

Compiled by Angela R. Edwards

CLARENCE JORDAN, JR.

    My God, My Protector 68

    My Guardian Angel at Work 70

MARVELL GALES

    Joy's Perfect Place 73

NIKKI DENISE

    For Chrissakes: I Was Just a Child! 81

SHANERICKA JONES

    Joy the World Didn't Give 85

CONCLUSION: GOD'S JOY IS FOR ALL 89

TELL GOD ALL ABOUT IT! 90

ABOUT THE COMPILER 95

CONTACT THE PUBLISHER 98

APPENDIX 99

Tondra "Poetic Sense" Mosley

Dedication:
I dedicate this moment in time to my beloved Angela Edwards, who exemplifies the very fiber of God's "Joy-Bearing Fruit." Thank you for being a nurturing seed and fruit that remains!

Bio:
Tondra "Poetic Sense" Mosley is an East St. Louis, Illinois native. A few of her accomplishments include: International Best-Selling Author, Speaker, Facilitator, Poet, and Plus-Size Model. For over 20 years, she has spoken and performed on platforms such as the St. Louis Bar Association, Black Woman's Caucus, and NAACP. Her literary endeavors include the publication of her book, Poetically Speaking: Volume 1, and numerous contributions to other works. Tondra is certified as a Human Behavior Science Consultant, Sexual Assault & Rape Advocate, and Suicide & Crisis Educator. Connect with her online by visiting www.poeticsense.net.

Compiled by Angela R. Edwards

God's JOY-Bearing Fruit – A Poem
Tondra "Poetic Sense" © 2020

I remember one day I took a bite.
I opened wide the mouth of my thoughts
and partook of its nectar delight.
My eyes of discernment perceived an awakening like none other.
It called out to me like a beckoning call of a once lovesick lover.
I felt neither tempted nor threatened nor pressured adieu.
Yet I felt excitingly afraid and, at the same time, safely secured.
I entrusted my taste buds, where I had no trace.
I yielded over what was natural knowledge just for a spiritual base.
I found myself consumed, convinced, convicted, and converted
By a fruit that yielded rapidly reproducing seeds
that made biting blindly well worth it.
The more I partake of this fruit, the more its nectar reveals
That this is a fruit that only the **JOY** of the Lord seals.
I recognized He takes good pleasure in my trust in His being,
Eating of a fruit biting beyond what's perceived,
as seeing is believing.
This fruit bears sensory trajection before experiencing its formation.
God's **JOY** fruit is your faith; in His every word, personification.
That word not only includes the promises He made to you,
But trusting and believing in the greatness
He spoke into the very creation of you, too.
This **JOY** fruit that I speak is the flushing out of your
perception of what's encapsulated in a seed.
It is the living life in total confidence that Thee,
all in all, is all within me.

Angela R. Edwards

Dedication:

I dedicate my **JOY** story to my grandchildren: Aniyah, Kelyce, Porter, and Dakota. They bring me *so* much **JOY**!

Bio:

Angela R. Edwards is a New Jersey native now residing in Texas. She is the CEO and Chief Editorial Director of Pearly Gates Publishing and Redemption's Story Publishing, both which are Award-Winning International Best-Selling Publishing Houses and A+-rated with the Houston Better Business Bureau. As a domestic violence survivor, she works tirelessly to assist both victims and survivors of abuse by helping to give voice to their plights in the *God Says I am Battle-Scar Free* book series. Angela is married to James Edwards and is the mother of two and grandmother of four. She lives by her motto: *"My Words Have **POWER**!"*

Compiled by Angela R. Edwards

Seven, Seven, Seven Years

I find it most fitting that my parents named me "Angela." The very essence of the name speaks of **JOY**. At every turn, the meaning behind my name is "Angel; Angelic." What are angels most often associated with? Glorifying and magnifying God all day, every day, in Heaven!

My story speaks of a time when I wasn't **JOY**ful…when I didn't have the strength to praise my way through the storm like I was trained and knew how to do.

Coming off the heels of an abusive marriage some 20+ years ago, my self-esteem was at an all-time low. I didn't know who I was; neither did I know what was next for me. During the marriage, I had (admittedly) strayed away from my Christian roots, making it all the more difficult to regain my footing in what I knew God said about me.

So, I needlessly suffered.

At the time, I thought that being in the arms of a new man would heal my broken heart and spirit. After a short spell of being hopelessly alone, I erroneously connected with someone who was eerily similar to the "situation" from which I had removed myself. The *primary* difference between the two was that my new beau never put his hands on me in an offensive way. Other than that critical aspect of our relationship, I soon learned that he, too, was a functioning addict…*JUST* like my ex.

What in the world? **NO WAY!** He was, after all, a "Preacher's Kid"! He knew better! *(Who here knows that the enemy goes after them harder than "the norm"?)*

I somehow managed to look past that (again) and did what I knew how to: *LOVE* with all my heart. However, there was a major problem that nestled into the depths of my soul: I was giving **ALL** my love to a man and not God. Surely, there would be a hefty price to pay for that!

For seven years, on and off, my new beau and I were at war. I loved him. I hated him. I wanted him. I broke up with him. Then, the cycle repeated…**FOR SEVEN YEARS!** It was a draining experience—one I would never wish on my worst enemy. At every turn, my **JOY** was sapped out of my very soul. No matter how hard I tried to regain my strength to move on once and for all, I was drawn back into his arms. I believe I was still dealing with the verbal abuse dished out by my ex-husband. Those words, *"Nobody else is going to want you,"* reverberated through my mind each time I thought I would break free from the stronghold.

Yes, someone else **DID** want me…but for what?

I could never quite understand at the time what my beau wanted with damaged goods. Did he see me coming from a mile away? Did his spirit-man know my spirit-woman was yearning for love and was weak? I find it hard to accept anything else!

Life went on, as it always does. I remained a hot *MESS* of a woman who grappled with the loss of her identity. I cannot and do not place the blame on anyone but myself, though. I knew better than to rely on anyone—let alone a man—to bring genuine **JOY** into my life. Sadly, God *seemed* so far away because of the choices I made to set Him aside.

One of the hardest lessons in life for me was embracing God's Agape Love when I was "going through." I often felt the familiar tug that would lead me back to His throne, but I fought against it. I have no good excuse, but I have a reason:

I believed I was unworthy. WRONG!

Let's look at what God's Word says about why I was *SO* inaccurate in my thinking:

> *"I have loved you with an everlasting love;*
> *I have drawn you with unfailing kindness."*
> (Jeremiah 31:3)

Wait. What? **GOD** loved *ME* with an **EVERLASTING** love?! (It's a personal thing. Yes, God loved *ME*!)

It was in **THAT** space where, after **SEVEN YEARS**, I remembered there was a love greater than any man's—just for *ME*. All that I yearned for wasn't found in my beau after **SEVEN YEARS** (I still find it hard to believe at times that I endured for *THAT* long). Only God's everlasting love could (and did) bring me the **JOY** I sought after in the wrong place for one too many times.

Once I released myself from the toxicity of what I *thought* was true love, I gained immeasurable **JOY** in the Lord! That is the lesson I want you, Dear Reader, to learn. We are commanded to not love anything nor anyone more than God (Exodus 20:3). We should not have the expectation that people, places, or things can bring us **JOY**. They may give us temporary *happiness*, but there is a stark difference between **JOY** and **HAPPY**, although they are often used interchangeably:

"The world" defines **JOY** as: "A feeling of great pleasure."

"The world" defines **HAPPY** as: "Feeling or showing pleasure or contentment."

JOY, my friend, is more than a moment in time and more than any one circumstance (those are qualifiers for *happiness*). As Christians, we can easily relate to **JOY** as being a deep abiding and settled state of hope and confidence.

After **SEVEN YEARS**, I realized *THAT* was what I was seeking…that "thing" that was missing in my life. What are you missing that only **JOY'S** *PEACE* (given by God Almighty) can fulfill? Please don't wait **SEVEN YEARS** — let alone another day. Get your **JOY** today!

Compiled by Angela R. Edwards

Marlowe R. Scott

Dedication:

Praising Jesus Christ for being the **JOY** of my salvation and messages I am blessed to share through Angela Edwards — my daughter — for par excellence support of my literary efforts.

Bio:

Marlowe Scott's God-given talents include authoring eight Best-Selling inspirational books, composing poetry, sewing, and crocheting. She shares Jesus' **JOY** through her writings and craftwork, to include inspirational pillows and quilts. Her continual prayer is that others find and accept Jesus Christ as their personal Savior, experience the **JOY** found through salvation, and grow in their Christian walk.

God's Joy Fruit

Joy - My Found Answer

****

Joy Deep Down in My Soul

A poem inspired © October 16, 2019

By Marlowe R. Scott

Many may say, "The **JOY** of the **LORD** is my strength,"
Because for the saved and redeemed, it surely is!
No matter the pains, disappointments, and problems,
Deep within, we know God can solve them.
As hymn and spiritual writers through the years
Have penned salvation's blessed story,
Those words of strength reinforce
The everlasting joys awaiting us in Glory!
Yes, yes, yes—the **JOY** of the **LORD** is **MY STRENGTH!**
No one can make me doubt it—
For the Holy Scriptures proclaim **LOUD** and **CLEAR**
With the **JOY** in **MY SOUL**,
*"The Savior Jesus Christ is **ALWAYS** near!"*

****

Compiled by Angela R. Edwards

When thinking about **JOY**, the first thing that came to my mind was the well-known Christmas carol, "Joy to the World." Why, you might ask?

As a Christian, that carol is the fulfillment of biblical prophecies. It was a truly blessed day when Jesus Christ, the Son of the Living God, was born in Bethlehem.

Before getting into further explanations, the words to "Joy to the World" are shared. It was first published in 1719 in a collection by the well-known author of many hymns, Isaac Watts.

Verse 1:

Joy to the world! The Lord is come;

Let Earth receive her King!

Let every heart prepare Him room,

And Heaven and nature sing,

And Heaven and nature sing,

And Heaven, and Heaven, and nature sing.

Verse 2:

Joy to the world! The Savior reigns;

Let men their songs employ!

While fields and floods, rocks, hills, and plains

Repeat the sounding joy,

Repeat the sounding joy,

Repeat, repeat the sounding joy.

Verse 3:

No more let sin and sorrows grow,

Nor thorns infest the ground.

He comes to make His blessings flow,

Far as the curse is found,

Far as the curse is found,

Far as, far as the curse is found.

Verse 4:

He rules the world with truth and grace,

And makes the nations prove

The glories of His righteousness;

And wonders of His love,

And wonders of His love,

And wonders, and wonders of His love.

Most people remember Christmas from their childhood — a day filled with expectations of gifts and treats of cookies, cakes, and pies…just to start. There were glittering decorations, visits with family and friends, parties, and, for some, the expectation of a visit from Santa Claus or St. Nicholas. Of course, there are numerous other traditions observed with different cultures throughout the world.

Through the years, I have learned the *true* meaning of Christmas (for many Christians, it's also known as the Advent season). The true meaning of the holiday is **NOT** the things and activities usually associated with it, especially in the world we live in today. Sadly, "the world" gives Jesus Christ a backseat while the worldly desires of mankind overshadow the holiday's significance.

In college English composition classes, I learned that important facts should be toward the front of the subject being written about. With the Fruit of the Spirit's second word being **JOY**, I believe its placement after **LOVE** is no accident! It is easy to know that after you experience the type of **LOVE** given through Jesus Christ, you will definitely have **JOY**...**never ending JOY!**

Joy and happiness are often interchanged, with many considering them to mean the same. In reality, **JOY** is stronger than happiness. A few words that may be more suitable to be interchanged with joy are:

- Delight
- Jubilation
- Triumph
- Exultation
- Rejoicing
- Gladness
- Tranquility
- Glee
- Exhilaration
- Bliss
- Rapture

JOY is about inner peace and contentment. **JOY** is lasting!

Examples of joy might include the birth of a baby or when one becomes saved by receiving Jesus Christ as their personal Savior. The "high" experienced by salvation cannot be explained in words! Other spiritual **JOY** experiences are those blessings we receive that are unexplainable, overflowing, and humbling.

Psalm 126:3 states simply, *"The LORD hath done great things for us; whereof, we are glad."*

Conversely, happiness is often temporary — an outward expression of elation. For example, amid a birthday party, where the celebration typically involves receiving gifts, eating delicious foods, and enjoying ourselves, something happens to disrupt the happiness. Suddenly, there are hurt feelings, personality conflicts, and (commonplace in today's world) fights and even killings!

Wedding anniversaries are celebrated if the marriage lasts and is not weakened by infidelity, abuse, or other conflicts. We get happy when promoted or earn educational achievements and degrees. However, in time, we want more education or a position with a higher salary.

*"I have no greater **JOY** than to hear that my children walk in truth"* (3 John 4:4 — emphasis added).

Now, I will **NOT** get into that age-old argument asserted by some about December 25th not being the day Jesus Christ was born. That is not an issue for me. The truth of the matter is that Jesus Christ of Nazareth was *BORN* as a babe in a stable. He had an animal feeding trough for His first bed. Jesus was born of a virgin named Mary and was raised as the son of a carpenter named Joseph — as was prophesied.

At Jesus' birth, the heavens rejoiced! A choir of angels sang and announced the birth of the Promised Messiah to shepherds in the fields at night.

As Jesus grew and walked this Earth, He felt and experienced hurts, being lied about, jealousy by religious leaders, and doubts of his Lordship by His close circle of the first 12 disciples. Those things culminated in His life by the final insult: The Son of God was crucified on an old rugged cross — one He had to carry Himself up Calvary Hill to be hung between two criminals!

As the fourth verse of "Joy to the World" states: *"He rules the world with truth and grace; He makes the nations prove the glories of His righteousness and wonders of His love."* How could a Savior such as Jesus Christ give **JOY** to anyone with an end like that? Well, the answer is simple:

THE CROSS WAS NOT THE END!

On the third day, after being crucified, Jesus Christ rose triumphantly from the grave, walked the Earth, and was seen by many whose testimonies are recorded in the Holy Bible! On the preordained day, Jesus then transcended to Heaven to dwell until His return (as recorded in the Book of Revelation).

BUT, being the loving, compassionate Savior of our souls, the Comforter (or Holy Spirit (the third person of the Trinity)) was left here with us on Earth!

CONCLUSION

Personally, I find a deep connection with God's creation. For me, there's peace and contentment when I hear the birds chirp and watch the deer in the field, rabbits hopping across the yard, and chipmunks scampering on the gazebo and posing on the rocks. In summation, nature gives me the **JOYFUL** feeling of tranquility.

Each day in 2019, I was led to both read and listen to Psalm 16 on my tablet. This soothing psalm had a beautiful message, just as so many others do. Verse 11 states, *"Thou wilt shew me the path of life: in thy right hand, there are pleasures forevermore."* Those pleasures are surely encompassed in the saying, ***"The JOY of the LORD is MY STRENGTH!"***

Among my list of many ***JOYS*** in my life was the blessing of authoring seven inspirational books. One has been published as a trilogy of the first three, and the last is a children's book encouraging children and adults alike to learn their ancestry. The titles are:

- *Spiritual Growth: From Milk to Strong Meat*
- *Believing Without Seeing: The Power of Faith*
- *Keeping It Real: The Straight and Narrow*
- *Worth the Journey: The Train Ride to Glory (trilogy)*
- *"I AM" Cares: His Eyes Are on the Sparrow*
- *Never Alone: Intimate Times with Jesus*
- *Plentiful Harvest: Fertile Ground*
- *Talli's Ancestry Surprise: Beginning the Ancestral Search*

The books are available on Amazon or through the publisher's website at www.PearlyGatesPublishing.com.

Compiled by Angela R. Edwards

Laurie Benoit

Dedication:
*To all those who have carried far too much for far too long:
It's time to let go and find your own... Journey to Joy.*

Bio:
Laurie Benoit is a mother, wife, and grandmother who resides in the village of Climax, Saskatchewan, where she has rekindled her love for writing. With the release of her book, *The Transformative Power of "The Word"* in 2019, and as a Contributing Author in *God Says I am Battle-Scar Free: Testimonies of Abuse Survivors – Parts 4 & 5* and *God's Love Fruit: Walking Through the Fields of Grace and Mercy in Bloom*, Laurie has become an International Best-Selling Author and Mentor. It is her wish to inspire others to discover their own Journey to Joy.

A Journey to Joy

"With Gratitude, Self-Love, and Acceptance Comes Joy for Life."
© 2019 Author Laurie Benoit @ Once Awakened
www.facebook.com/onceawakened

Joy (noun): A feeling of great pleasure and happiness.

I must admit: *Joy* is **not** something that has made an entrance into my days throughout my life very often. In fact, at nearly 50 years of age, I am only truly beginning to understand what Joy *really* feels like. I suppose it's better late than never, right?

Early on in my life, the closest I came to experiencing what Joy felt like and meant was when I gave birth to each of my children. It was, however, a feeling that was short-lived. Now, believe me when I say I adore and love the beautiful little beings that came from me. The very moment I saw and held them was genuinely joyful. Then, as life would have it, I "forgot" that feeling until the next time to give birth arrived. In my in-between moments of Joy, each helped me move forward into the woman I am now working on becoming.

Admittedly, our journeys are sometimes burdened with many challenges that aid us in becoming the person we are meant to be. If someone would have told me that years ago, I would have either gotten angry or laughed and said, *"What a load of malarkey!"* Sadly, the truth of the matter is that it has taken me a great many years to learn that truth.

Still... There are moments from my past I would have gladly traded for just a slither of happiness and Joy. I have lived a life of abuse, neglect, substance abuse, depression, and suicidal thoughts and tendencies.

In my 40s, when I really wanted to apply *The Law of Attraction* to my life, I felt like I was unable to achieve one of the most important steps: **Manifestation**. Everything I read about it kept repeating these exact words:

See it, feel it, and believe it to achieve it.

Well, that told me what? Nothing, really.

Many people who are considered "leaders" and have the knowledge of The Law of Attraction literally charge hundreds of dollars—**JUST** to share their "SECRET" as to what a person needs to do to achieve manifestation. As with most things I've learned in my life, I learned it almost exclusively on my own. I did, however, read one book that offered me some clarity. The truth about manifestation is actually simple: Whatever you desire to do, set your mind to doing it, believe in yourself while you're doing it, and you can achieve your goals! Simple, right? Follow your heart and do the one thing that you alone are meant to do. Believe me when I say we all have a purpose in life, and it's not to just work, pay bills, and die.

Through my learning process, I came across a social media page that really made me think about something I had been missing my entire life: the feeling of **GRATITUDE**. See, my life was such a whirlwind of one shitstorm after another, leaving me to feel as if I had nothing for which to be grateful—but I did! That revelation was one of the most monumental and life-changing moments for me.

Now, you might be thinking: How can a person go through life and not feel gratitude?

Well, if **YOUR** life was *anything* like mine, you might be able to understand. For many years, I simply didn't see anything to be grateful for in my life, aside from my children. I didn't have much in the way of family, no truly stable relationships or friendships, and the stable friends were a great distance away.

I consistently found myself in abusive situations and always carried my dark, silent friend called "Depression" with me. Believe me when I tell you that gratitude does not exist in that place of darkness.

So, I began to explore what gratitude felt like. I started feeling and expressing my appreciation for those things many take for granted — the very sight I am so very fortunate to have now and have had my entire life; my ability to walk and spend time in nature's beauty; my sense of smell; my ability to hear and speak clearly; and even other small things such as a meal on the table, clean clothing, and a roof over my head. I then realized my "Gratitude List" kept growing! The more I began to see all I had indeed been blessed with, the more blessings came!

Along with those feelings of gratitude came feelings of **JOY**!

Why had it taken me so long to see how truly blessed I am? I can tell you why. Because I was in a place where life was **ALL** about what I didn't have and not what I *DID* have. Because I was in a place where I hadn't done the work I was supposed to and needed to do. Because I let all the negativity in my life run over me like a freight train stopping and backing up to rerun the same piece of track. Because pain was what I felt in the very deepest pits of my heart and soul. Those reasons and more are my "why."

You can't feel JOY and GRATITUDE *when you barely feel anything at all.*

So, in my 40s, my journey began. I started writing, healing, crying many, many tears, and learning more about myself. I had to learn to accept myself for all my flaws—and oh, my goodness…I have a whole **LOT** of them!

Then, when I wasn't looking for or in expectation of anything new in my life, something else was sent to me through the universe…

An article I read added even **more** clarity to my life! It was something I truly and desperately needed. I have it saved even now so that I can reflect on it as I work more on myself over passing time. I have also shared it with others because I'm *certain* they may need it, too. Now, let me explain the 'why'…

See, there is one saying that has always really aggravated me more than any other: *"Forgive and forget."* Just forgive…and forget. Okay, but can someone please tell me **HOW TO**?! I never had anyone to look up to in life, so how in the *HELL* does a person do it?! Not a single person I have **EVER** asked gave me a real explanation—not even the doctors I used to see for my depression! So, what… **Was I supposed to "just know"?**

Back to the article…

I took the time to read every single word, and **WOW**! Someone actually made a real effort to explain the "Forgive and Forget" process. I was genuinely grateful for that. I clearly understood what the writer expressed, and someone finally provided the answer about **HOW** to forgive! Thank you!!!

Then, it began. That one piece helped me begin to forgive *some* of those who hurt me. It has also allowed me to forgive myself and alleviate some of the heaviness in my own heart for what I've imposed on others. For me, forgiveness is an ongoing learning process. Undeniably, I still have a long way to go before I am ready to forgive some who've caused me pain. *Perhaps one day, forgiveness for them will come...*

I must admit there are still days when I am challenged with staying focused on gratitude and forgiveness. After all, let's face it: On any given day, we never know what we may encounter.

What I **can** tell you with surety is this: When we remember to be grateful, life sends us more to be grateful for. When we do our best to forgive another, we set ourselves free, too. That is where **self-love** comes in.

Because my life had been filled with negativity and self-loathing from all I had endured, words of pain and hurt from others resonate through the recesses of my mind — even now, at times. Even during the best of times, it's challenging to silence those voices, but with a bit of help from gratitude and forgiveness, I learned the value of self-love. When I began to realize I would never live up to other people's standards, I found more acceptance of myself. When I began to forgive myself, I realized how imperfectly perfect I am. I am human. I feel. I make mistakes. I have hurt others (and will probably continue to do so—whether intentionally or unintentionally). I am the only person who knows what I feel at any given time. Only I know what makes my heart sing!

So, why was I not doing the things I love? What was I waiting for? Well, I can tell you this one thing: I was always waiting for *"when I get older…when the kids grow up…when I get my education…when I…"* I'm sure you get the picture.

I am not waiting for anything or anyone anymore! Right now—at this moment—I deserve to do things that make me love life…and myself. I love my family and friends, and I love those who have joined me on my journey. I want them to be joyful, too! Frankly, I have had enough of not living life the way it should have been so many years ago. I am the one who is in control of my destiny, and I have decided that **MY** life is going to be as beautiful as I choose it to be.

It has already been many years since I began my "reconstructive journey," and I am certain there are still many more years ahead. Like everyone else, I, too, face one moment at a time, one day at a time, and one year at a time. I will say this, though: I will do **everything** in my power to love each day in the best possible ways I can. Yes, I will face challenges. Some days will be harder than others. Nonetheless, I am willing to give each day my best, and that is the most one can do!

I'm happy to report that Joy is more commonplace in my days now ever since I began rediscovering my inner child through my photography. You might be thinking, *"Yeah…yeah. Okay, Laurie. Photography? What are you talking about?"* However, I'd like you to think about the following…

Life through the eyes of a child is considerably different in comparison to adults. To them, anything and everything is possible. Their dreams are magnificent, bold, and free. They color so freely, creatively, and in shades adults "forget" that bring sunshine to our lives. Children look around them and find interest in **everything**. If you just sit with, listen with intent, or study a child's behavior when they are outside, you may catch a *small* glimpse of how they soak in **everything**. They pick up and notice every little miracle adults often overlook, all because we have become conditioned and outgrown our own wonder.

That is how I have been relearning to view my life.

For me, this story is just a small piece of what has brought Joy back into my life. I am trying to view the world with wonder, instead of with a heavy and sad heart for all I have lived through. I can honestly say I am finally finding my own peace and **JOY** in a world that has been anything but fair to me.

And so, I ask you this: *What are **YOU** waiting for?*

You deserve to be happy! Isn't it time you decided to be as well?

Compiled by Angela R. Edwards

Reyna Harris-Goynes

Dedication:

I dedicate this my story to my grandma Alma Harris and my cousins, Quinton Harris and Charles Ransom, III, for being a part of my life and leaving me with some awesome memories.

Bio:

Reyna Harris-Goynes is a wife and mother of five. Her husband and she recently established a clothing boutique and t-shirt printing business. With her sights set on mid-2020 as her goal, she hopes to have her business dealings where she desires, especially when her husband goes to work and the primary responsibility rests with her. Be on the lookout for "V.R. Fashions & More"!

Life's Ultimate Joy

Life often throws you through so many loops; however, yearning for better will always bring you closer to your goal.

There's no denying the fact that people live…and people die. Some deaths are unexpected, leaving us unprepared for the sudden loss. When someone you're close to passes away, that loss can break you down in more ways than one. You may even want to shut yourself off from the rest of the world for a little while as you go through the grieving process.

When my grandma passed away in 2001, I saw the event a few days before it happened. While I was dreaming about her, she came to me in my dream and woke me up out of my sleep. I truly believe she made sure to visit me that way because I think she knew it was a possibility I wasn't going to be at the hospital "that day." My grandma was my everything and more. She was one of a kind and irreplaceable. I fondly recall her house as being "the place to be" daily, even for the other kids in the neighborhood. Grandma was always cooking and baking something for us, too. When she was in the kitchen, I was there as well—watching and learning.

In 2013, my cousin died in a car accident on his way to Dallas, Texas. The roads were icy, and he and another driver lost control of their vehicles. He was pronounced dead on the scene. (As children, our grandma taught us to stick together like sisters and brothers, although we were, in fact, cousins.) His passing really hurt my family in ways we can't explain, to the point that many of us are still grieving. Thankfully, being able to recall happy times with him enables us to keep on pressing on. The love we had for him will never die. **Never.**

The year is now 2019. Another cousin lost his life to what we suspect was jealousy. He was killed by someone who was *supposed* to be his friend. (I cannot understand how a person can kill a person they claim is family!) Fortunately, there are moments of **JOY** that can be experienced, even after the loss. For example, if that person had children, the surviving family and friends get to watch them grow into adults. The deceased parent's legacy lives on through their children.

It's comforting when you recall the good times you had with your loved one. Conversely, you must remember not everyone is your friend. Some are only around to use you, so be cautious about who you let into your circle. Some people are there to reap all the benefits of your loyalty because they know you have a good heart. All the while, you must be strong—not only for yourself but your family as well…especially the children because they are likely struggling their way through grief and need the adults' support.

Since losing my cousin in 2013, I have been blessed to watch his children blossom into some fantastic kids and young adults who love their mom to the max. My cousin and his wife did an excellent job raising their children, even though they still struggle with him being gone so soon. I'm definitely praying that my other cousin's son turns out to be an awesome young man as well. I love the fact that all the children remind me in some way of their fathers. As they grow up, they truly favor their paternal sides of the family (in my opinion) in more ways than I could have imagined.

God's Joy Fruit

We never know how the loss of a parent could affect a child not only early in life, but also later in life. Sometimes, it can affect the child when they go to school that shows up in the form of having problems learning or even focusing on their work. Personally, I don't know what it feels like to lose a parent or child, but I can imagine the pain one goes through when faced with that tragedy.

A fond memory I have is of seeing my little cousin in her prom dress and her preparing to walk across the stage to obtain her diploma. Both were major accomplishments—both achieved without her father in attendance. She looked so beautiful. I have no doubt my cousin was very proud and smiled down on her with a heart filled with **JOY**.

Amid the sadness, we still managed to experience some good times both in our youth and as adults.

I recall how much I used to hate when my cousin (the one who passed in 2013) popped up at my house unannounced. As I reflect on those times, I now see it was his special way of spending time with my children and me—especially when he made the journey from Dallas, Texas to the Houston area. When he passed away, I kept saying, *"He'll be back to visit. He's just up the road in Dallas."* When reality set in, I knew he was never coming to knock on my door unexpectedly ever again. The pain of my new reality was brutal.

Sometimes, the loss of family and friends is meant to be a wake-up call that reminds you of this one fact: Life is truly short. No matter what you go through, take one day at a time and live in the moment.

There were many times I wished I could bring my loved ones back from the dead, but then I would stop and think, *"The way this world is nowadays, I'd rather not have them be subjected to everyday life such as it is!"* That doesn't stop me from missing them tremendously, though. I'm comforted in knowing they are smiling down on me and applauding how strong I've been these past few years with everything I've faced. I can't help but acknowledge how far I've come without the benefit of my family's full support—the kind I expected and was supposed to have. Since the loss of my grandma, I have learned so much over the years and adjusted to the constant changes in my life. One critical lesson I've learned is that not everyone has the same outlook on certain things that I do and, when they show their true colors, I should believe that's how they really feel—family or not. As a rule, we must be aware of those who are there to support you and those who are against you. There is always somebody waiting for your downfall. I encourage you to stay strong and focused on what you've been assigned to do.

I can still hear my grandma and cousins telling me, *"Reyna, we got you, baby! You got this! Keep pushing, no matter what is being said about you. Girl, you have some great ideas, and we want to see them come to fruition soon! For now, we're going to enjoy the ride together—**right now!**"* They spoke those words of encouragement as I worked to establish my business. Although I had my own business before, I had to put it on hold for a little while due to my living situation. I promised myself I would return to that venture in the years to come and incorporate it with my new business.

God's Joy Fruit

The **JOY** that I have is in knowing I've always had so much potential to be great; I just didn't know then how to use it to my advantage. My grandma's words keep me going.

"It's your time, baby!"

*"You and your husband have to put something out there and step out on **FAITH**."*

"Make it all work in your favor so that you'll have something to fall back on."

"You don't have to be successful; just get out there and start generating some income, regardless of what it is."

"Reyna, you have come so far from that depressed state you used to be in. It doesn't stop there, my dear. Keep on pushing until you get to where you need to be!"

No matter what I did in life, my grandma always had my back and so much faith in my abilities. I never had to try to please her because she was on my side (I suppose I made it easy for her because I rarely did anything wrong). I do, however, remember those times when she didn't want the neighborhood kids in her yard or was trying to get us to come inside, she would throw empty glass soda bottles out the door to get her point across. Another thing she did was teach us to use a little bit of salt on our watermelon to enhance the flavor. I took it to a whole other level and used it on **ALL** my fruit (everyone else used sugar on theirs). It's also peculiar to me at times when I see our family's children growing up doing some of the same things without us even telling them about the history. I have countless memories that flash through my mind any given moment that cause me to laugh aloud because they are hilarious.

I found **JOY** when I could finally think or talk about my lost loved ones without getting teary-eyed. The love I have for them is so strong and will remain that way forever. It wasn't too long ago when my heart would drop into my feet at the mere *thought* of them because it was hard to accept they were no longer here. I truly miss them every day but know they are in a better place and living it up together again. My grandma always held all her grandkids close to her heart. I am grateful to God for the time I had with her and for her teaching me the differences between right and wrong.

When she passed away, everyone took it hard, even though we knew it was her time to go. I owe so much of what I have accomplished to my grandma because she steered me onto the right path in life (except for the guys I chose to date). At times, things were difficult without the benefit of her guidance, but in my own way, I have learned to move on. I know she's proud of me, which means more than I can express here. Due to my grandma's diligence with sowing good seeds into my life, I proudly give myself props for the way my children's lives have turned out. Mistakes and all, each has found their own way on this life's journey.

Keeping my lost loved ones' memory alive is imperative, as I desire that they are never forgotten by **anyone**. I know they would do the same were it me who was no longer here. That's what family does! I love them all to infinity and beyond!

When my family is afforded the opportunity to sit around and reminisce about "the good old days," it brings me **GREAT JOY**! Although it's not easy dealing with loss, we must be mindful that God makes no mistakes. He is always working on our behalf and always on time…even when we least expect it. **HE BRINGS ME JOY!**

Compiled by Angela R. Edwards

Tosha R. Dearbone

Dedication:
In writing this story, God placed on my heart that it is for anyone feeling like life happened and they are not understanding that JOY can be their peace.

Bio:
Tosha R. Dearbone is a Louisiana native and raised in Houston, Texas. She is a mother of four and grandmother of one. Her professional achievements include: Medical Assistant, Certified Nursing Assistant, Certified Community Health Worker, Author, HIV and AIDS Advocate, and Founder of "Positive Express" — an organization that veers to young girls about self-esteem and educates them about other awarenesses. To connect with her, you can find her on all social media sites at Positive Express.
Website: www.trdearbo.wix.com/positiveexpress

Mirrors Don't Lie

Looking back over my life, I can remember a time when, for me to really experience joy, I had to turn the mirror around. Life experiences were staring me down, leaving me feeling unworthy of receiving **JOY**. Instead, I was left feeling as though I was a "mistake." I cried...and I cried as I pondered over this one thing: *How could my life be so overwhelming?*

It was self-evaluation time! Let me set up the scene:

I was a woman who viewed myself in the mirror and began to see a cracked woman with many bandages covering every type of wound imaginable. I had been sexually, verbally, and physically abused. Rejection, suicidal thoughts and tendencies, and low self-esteem stared back at me. I asked myself, *"How did I get here?"* The moment the mirror's cracked reflection looked back at my brokenness, I noticed things about myself—to include how not only did I allow the world to tear me down, but also those issues I have cast upon myself.

The degrading words that were spoken.

The pills.

The cycles of abuse.

Promiscuous behaviors.

The devaluing of my self-worth.

And...and...and...

Everything seemed to somehow weigh down on me all at once.

My own words no longer aligned with God's words that told me, *"I am fearfully and wonderfully made"* and that *"I can do all things through Christ, who gives me strength."* What I both felt in the depths of my soul and spoke into the atmosphere was, *"I can never do anything right."* I beat myself down because I had no one affirming me…no one to ensure Tosha was alright.

You know how you can be there for everyone else, but no one is there for you? That was me. Those whom I thought **should** be there simply were not.

So, as I suffered from all my "ills," the pills came into play. I figured if I left this world, no one would even care. I tried to overdose not once, but **THREE** times. I recall screaming aloud with frustration at my failed attempts, but no one was there to hear me. I was alone. It was not a good feeling!

As I got older, I entered relationship after relationship because I assumed being with anyone was better than being alone (I was looking for happiness for all the wrong reasons and in all the wrong ways). I guess that's what "they" call being promiscuous or, better yet, "fast"—as our elders would say. LOL! Before I knew it, I was in a lowly place; a place of expectations where I just knew good things were not going to happen for me.

Years flew by, and I knew in my heart that all I had encountered did not define me. I had to be the one to find my way up and out of my circumstances. So, I began to do some soul-searching. I read book after book, listened to podcasts, dissected God's Word a little bit stronger, and changed the way I viewed myself. Did I still have discouraging moments? Of course, I did! This was no overnight healing event, but rather a lifestyle change that needed to be made. I was in for a ride!

I needed to retrain my thoughts, look at the situations I found myself in, and really learn how to simply be happy. Being joyful seemed so far out of reach but was a necessity.

Little did I know I was being introduced to **JOY** when I attended church with my friend and her mother. I knew I felt different coming out than I did going in. In all honesty, I was unaware of what I would encounter when I walked through those church doors that day. Well, I continued attending services, and, one day, I felt this warm feeling on the inside. It was as if I was being lit on fire by sparks that radiated throughout my body. I wanted to run, scream, and shout!

You guessed it correctly if you said, *"She met the Holy Spirit that day!"* It was a new and unfamiliar feeling—and I **LOVED** it!

Each Sunday that came, I encountered that same feeling. I had the urge to share my great news, but with who? Who would understand what I was feeling? Why was it that I had no one with whom to share my **JOY**? Was it because the people in my life made me feel as though I were an outcast? *(I suppose I will never know.)* So, I remained quiet.

Then, one day, life began to seem clearer, and positivity's light shone through! I no longer beat myself down. Instead, I had an attitude shift, children to care for, and I no longer felt like what was going on around me or in my past mattered. I started to love **ME**—flaws and all! My new journey had begun.

In 2009, I joined my first church, "Morning Star." Although I had attended the church for years, I finally decided I would call it my church home. **BUT GOD!** I still felt like I needed **MORE**, so I decided to branch off and venture out on my own. One instance led me to listen to a teleconference on a Friday at noon. The pastor who preached the Word that day spoke to **ME**. I knew in my spirit I just *HAD* to visit his church, so I did. I hadn't taken the time to pray and think things through, though. I did not consider that I was leaving one church (where my soul was regularly being fed) to attend another with some level of uncertainty…

For a while, everything was going fine until one day, there was a misunderstanding. I had no idea what "church hurt" was, so I fell silent. Meanwhile, I kept seeing messages on social media about people experiencing church hurt, which caused me to ask myself, *"Could this be what's wrong with me?"* Well, yes it was! Talk about disappointed! I stopped going to church for a couple of months altogether, even after reaching out to my new pastor and receiving no response. I then decided to really seek God and ask HIM what I should do.

As the days ticked by, I watched online services with Pastor John Gray, Pastor Sarah Jakes-Roberts and her husband, Pastor Tour'e Roberts, and Pastor T.D. Jakes.

Wait. What is it that I was feeling? It was familiar and uncomfortable. I was not being fulfilled. Without a shadow of a doubt, I knew I needed to be in the **PRESENCE** of worship, teaching, and fellowship. I remember falling to my knees and crying out to God, *"God, PLEASE help me to feel adequate again! Show me where I am supposed to be!"* **HE** responded immediately and gave me a vision of one word:

TRANSFORMING.

With me not knowing what that meant, I just brushed it off.

Words of Knowledge: *Never brush off even the simplest of things such as one-word statements because it can easily be your "next level" or blessing.*

After watching the service that day, I flipped through my Facebook timeline and came across a page that I recognized. It was a man I knew as "The Confidence Coach" from Periscope (another online platform). I paused my scrolling and started paying close attention to what he was talking about. At the time, he was having Sunday service at a church in Houston, Texas. Talk about stoked!

Let me go a bit deeper here. Remember that earlier in the day, I saw the word *"TRANSFORMING"*? Guess what? His church was named **"Transforming Faith Christian Center"**! WOW! God had given me a vision, and I had no idea at the time what it meant—but He *quickly* made it clear!

That following Sunday, I decided to get up and visit that church. When I tell you that upon my entrance, I felt right at home—I knew then I had **truly** arrived. I remember when service was over, and I was asked if I enjoyed the service, I didn't even hesitate with my response: *"It was **GREAT**! I will be back! Not just back; I will be **joining**!"* I was filled with so much **JOY** and excitement, I couldn't wait to share my testimony with others. I believe my close friend Natosha was the first person I told and how I knew the Pastor from Periscope. She was happy for me.

Fast-forward...

In October 2018, I joined what is now my church family. When I say the Word made me want to leap, grow, and truly increase in my personal relationship with God, it did just that! I have never been happier to be in a place surrounded by people with the same goal: to be used by **GOD**.

So, when I look back over my life, I can honestly see the **JOY** upon my life. It's always been there; I just needed to make sure He (GOD) was the Head and amid all that I was doing as my heart aligned with God's purpose for me. My **JOY** now comes from the inner me, and everything else flows freely, to include:

- Ministering to the young ladies in my organization, "Positive Express."
- Ministering on my job, into my children's and granddaughter's lives, and the young ladies in the Leadership Academy.

Each instance and opportunity to sow into them is in full alignment with what keeps my **JOY** at "one hundred." Each day, it feels like a miracle that was destined to happen. I just had to turn the mirror around and truly focus on **ME**. There's no more beating myself up or trying to commit suicide. I can honestly say my self-esteem is balanced. I love **ME**, and I hope that as you have read my story, you, too, will turn the mirror around and look within to see exactly from where your joy flows.

JOY flows from your positioning in Christ. Ask yourself, *"Who am I in Him?"* and then listen carefully for His reply.

God's Joy Fruit

A prayer that kept me afloat most recently is one "Positive Express" uses with the young ladies within the Leadership Academy called *The Knots Prayer*.

"Dear God, please untie the knots that are in my mind, my heart, and my life. Remove the have-nots, the can-nots, and the do-nots that I have in my mind. Erase the will-nots, may-nots, and might-nots that may find a home in my heart. Release me from the could-nots, would-nots, and should-nots that obstruct my life. And most of all, Dear God, I ask that you remove from my mind, my heart, and my life all the "am-nots" that I have allowed to hold me back, especially the thought of "I am not good enough." Amen.

(Author Unknown)

Compiled by Angela R. Edwards

CaTina Jenkins

Dedication:
I dedicate my story to my wonderful mother, Johnnie May Bursey. I've always admired your amazing strength. I wish I could give you the world. I thank and love you, Momma!

Psalm 30:5
"For His anger endureth but a moment; in His favour is life: weeping may endure for a night, but JOY cometh in the morning."

After the Pain

The death of a loved one is the worst pain ever. The pain I felt after my grandma's passing did a real number on me. I was so depressed, yet everyone around me thought I was fine. I asked my doctor for medication to help with my depression, and she said, *"You don't need anything; just give it some time."*

The passing of my grandma was the beginning of my journey down the wrong path. Every time I listen to the song "Don't Worry About Me," I think about her.

I remember seeing her laying in that hospital bed. She was in so much pain, and the doctors had given up on her. Cancer was taking over her body, and her kidneys had started to fail. The doctor called for an emergency family meeting to see if we wanted to approve her for surgery to try to remove the cancer from her colon or if we wanted to just let her go in peace. That was a very difficult decision to make; however, I couldn't see myself choosing to have my grandma endure more pain. After all, surgery wasn't going to help because the cancer had already started spreading throughout her body. As a family, we decided against her having the procedure.

I called my grandma's pastor, and he came to the hospital to pray for her. I recall seeing the tears fall from my grandma's eyes, which prompted a flood of tears of my own. I said to her, *"Grandma, if you're tired and you're ready to go home, it's okay. Don't worry about me. I'm going to be alright."* I didn't know at the time if that was my **truth**, but those were the words that felt right at that moment. I then told her, *"I'll be back to see you when I get off work tonight."*

Later that day, the call came that she had passed away. Getting that phone call while I was at work felt as if someone had stabbed me in my heart. All I kept saying was, ***"She didn't wait for me... She didn't wait for me..."***

Shortly after grandma's death, I strayed from the church. Every time I went to church, I would cry because I felt empty and alone without her. Eventually, I just stopped going altogether. I was angry with my family, everybody else...and God. I couldn't understand how my and the pastor's prayers didn't keep her alive — at least long enough for me to be by her side when she transitioned.

As a result of my straying from what I knew I was right, I started drinking and partying a **LOT** — something I never did before. Before my grandma's passing, I wasn't into the club and drinking scene whatsoever. My life had indeed changed.

In 2016, the Angel of Death visited my world yet again. I had just dropped off a friend and, within minutes, received a call that he was on his way to the hospital. On my way to see him, I prayed for God to save him. I arrived at the hospital, only to discover that he had just passed away. I was so hurt. I started drinking every day just to go to sleep and find some level of inner peace.

That negative sphere of indulgence went on for a while until the day I picked up my Bible again. At that moment, my healing journey began. God took all the pain I felt and replaced it with **JOY**. Other times when I felt better were when I listened to gospel songs or a sermon. Still, something was missing. I had yet to step back into the house of the Lord. I cannot explain how I knew, but I believe God was preparing me for the pain HE knew I was going to endure in the next year to come.

On July 21, 2018, my Uncle Mike passed away *(he was actually my mother's cousin, but he lived with my grandma, so my children and I were taught to call him our uncle)*. We were very close. Uncle Mike was like the father my children didn't have. He spoiled them and treated them as his own. He instilled a lot of positive things into them for their future. Needless to say, I was ***devastated*** when he passed away. That time, however, because my faith in the Word had gotten stronger, I was genuinely okay and didn't respond as I had previously.

Six months later, I lost my sister, Phyllis, on my daughter's birthday. On January 27, 2019, my sister passed out unexpectedly and without any apparent reason. For five days, she remained on life support with no brain activity. We weren't prepared to let her go; however, **someone** had to make a decision that would bring closure. I felt like the only fair thing to do was to allow her children to decide what it was they wanted to do. It was tough watching my sister's sons struggle with the decision to end their mom's life. I clearly remember my sister saying, *"If I have to live and depend on someone else to care for me, I don't want to live that way."* In the end, we set our feelings to the side and honored her request. Keeping her alive just to satisfy our needs would have been selfish. On the day she was removed from life support, she continued to breathe on her own for four hours. That gave us hope that she would pull through, but we did come to accept that if she didn't, it was the Lord's will, and He was ready for her.

Sometime later, one of my sister's sons left the room to get some food. It seemed as if she waited for him to reappear before taking her last breath. Shortly after his return, she exhaled, opened her eyes, closed them, and then passed away with a smile on her face. No longer was she in pain. No longer was she suffering. My sister was at peace.

The pain I felt from my sister's passing was much harder for me to recover from, but I prayed daily for God to give me the strength to be resilient for my family. My mother and my sister's five children needed me...

My sister and I were very close. It's still hard to imagine my life without her. We used to talk on the phone for **hours**, catching up on the latest gossip in town. LOL! I'm going to miss her 7:00 a.m. calls on birthdays—and not just **MY** birthday. Phyllis would call me on **EVERYONE'S** birthday! If she called someone and couldn't reach them, she would call me next just to tell me to let "such-and-such" know she tried to call to wish them a "Happy Birthday."

Even though Phyllis and I didn't have the same blood running through our veins, no one would know—unless they knew our history. My sister would always correct anyone who tried to say we **WEREN'T** sisters. People would say, *"Oh, that's the little girl your mom raised,"* and Phyllis would reply, *"No; this is my **SISTER**."*

After Phyllis died, I lost focus. Prior to her passing, I had just gone to class to get my license to start my new business. I was also preparing to sign the paperwork to close on my new house. I was so distraught, I just dropped the ball on everything. I also quit my job of six years. I was grieving on the inside and wouldn't let it out. Once again, I got angry with the world and began to shut down. Unlike before, however, I didn't turn to drinking (my usual coping mechanism) because I had long ago realized alcohol only ***temporarily*** numbed the pain; it didn't take it away.

On March 17, 2019 (it was a Sunday), I woke up and decided I needed to hear a word from God. I got dressed and went to church. That was the day that changed my life. That time, I didn't run from God: I ran **TO** Him. I knew from where my strength would come. *"Weeping may endure for a night, but **JOY** comes in the morning"* is a very true statement.

I still have moments when I'm alone and cry, but those tears are God's way of healing me and taking away the pain. Each tear that is shed, God replaces it with **JOY**...***HIS JOY!*** I feel **JOY** when I'm in church, praising Him, and even when I'm riding around in my car. He fills me up and strengthens me every day.

Somewhere, amid all the pain, suffering, and injustice, God is **always** working it out for our good and His glory. God uses trials to test our faith and to shape us into His perfect image, all while teaching us dependency on Him. It brings me great **JOY** to serve and talk about the goodness that God has brought into my life. I have been through some of the worst seasons of my life—times when I didn't think I would make it this far. Now, I see God moving and fulfilling His promises.

On August 5, 2019, I gave my life back to God and joined "The Fountain of Praise" church. **YES! I found a church home!** The favor that God has on my life is **AMAZING!** *Exceedingly* and *abundantly* are His promises, and He's honored them to the fullest. Once I gave my life back to God, doors started opening for me. He's positioned and connected me to people I *knew* but hadn't realized that they would one day sit at the same table with me. God has given me back my focus.

I now know that this whole time, God was permitting chaos in my life to get my attention and to show me that **HE** is the *ONLY* way. God took me—a "nobody"—and made me into **SOMEBODY**! He has given me a purpose in His Kingdom as one of His chosen.

God is not through with me yet!

Sathya Callender

Bio:

Sathya Callender is a Domestic Violence Advocate, Motivational Speaker, and Business Owner. As an advocate and speaker, she uses her passion to empower other women to be overcomers. She is the Owner of Kutie Patooties Gift Boutique, Founder of Scars of Survival, and has participated in other collaborative literary works. Sathya is the mother of five beautiful children.

Connect with Sathya at www.sathyacallender.com or sathya.callender@gmail.com.

Compiled by Angela R. Edwards

The JOY I Felt When...

You may suffer sorrow and pain on this side of Heaven, but **JOY** cometh in the morning! Just ask me! Following is my **"JOY"** story...

I thought I was experiencing true love, yet somehow found myself in an 18-month toxic relationship with a guy who hadn't gone through the healing process after a relationship that failed after 14 years. How, then, could he call himself loving me? I soon learned that the love I felt (or what appeared to be love) was nothing more than lust. On the surface, everything appeared to be so genuine between us—but that's why it's said, *"Looks can be deceiving."* Indeed, things may not always be what they seem.

A person can look you in the eyes and tell you how much they love you without sincerity. Perhaps those words are spoken to put you in a "comfortable place" with them. Have you ever heard the expression, *"Hurt people hurt people"*?

The man I thought loved me was still hurting and had yet to be completely healed from his pain. He was insecure, didn't know what unconditional love was, and didn't know how to give or receive love because he hadn't experienced reciprocated love in the past. He was raised to survive—and those lessons were not taught with love. Nonetheless, I grew to love him for who he was. I began showing him what I knew how to do: give love.

I invested time in trying to understand why he rejected my love. Why did he tell me not to show him? Why would anyone reject the love of their partner—the one they profess to love? Actions speak louder than words, correct?

As time progressed, I began to think I was a rebound and that all he wanted was someone to remove the thoughts of him being hurt in the past. Still, I knew the desires of **MY** heart. I knew what I wanted and needed, and that relationship wasn't fulfilling either. In response to all I was enduring, I started praying more than ever. I asked God to show me if the relationship was meant to be. *"God, what am I doing wrong? How could someone not want unconditional love?"* I asked.

I then began reflecting on different conversations my love and I had where he stated he had been cheated on, belittled, used, and abused. No wonder he was clueless about the benefits of unconditional love and why he rejected my love! I understood why he was insecure and lacked ambition. After gaining that understanding, I said to myself, *"Well, maybe I can continue to show him with my actions. He'll then understand and follow suit."* All I was doing, however, was pouring myself more and more into a toxic, broken relationship that wasn't meant to be. **That man needed to heal!**

Time went by, and God showed me signs that my 'love' wasn't who He had for me, yet I continued to allow my feelings to take over and wallow in guilt. I kept saying to God, *"But I love him so much!"* I kept feeling bad, but how could I feel that way for someone who didn't feel bad for himself? I continued to hold out hope that he would realize just how much I loved him.

My efforts were fruitless. I slowly lost the essence of myself while trying to prove something to a man who was blind to my love fruit. Of course, nothing changed. He remained a bitter, hurt man. The man I loved unconditionally didn't love me in return—period! What a hard pill to swallow after 18 months!

For 18 months, I remained in a stagnant relationship.

For 18 months, I tried to prove my love to a man who didn't know what real love was, even when it was right in his face.

Talk about one-sided! All he knew was what was in it for him. Forget about me; I was irrelevant.

It was time for self-evaluation and self-reflection. As I looked at myself in the mirror, I saw a beautiful queen who was full of intelligence, wisdom, knowledge, and had a whole *LOT* of love to give…to the right man. I began to rethink what "true love" really was. I knew it wasn't hurt, pain, and sorrow! Was I in a relationship that I wanted to continue dealing with? Was it what God truly desired for His beautiful daughter? **Absolutely not!** Although patience is truly a virtue and must be practiced, I believe that loving ourselves and our Heavenly Father is much more important than giving ourselves to others who are undeserving. We can't expect love from anyone if we don't love ourselves first.

Loneliness is something that can lead to toxic relationships, leaving us to "settle" when we know better. We must learn to set standards and know that the right man or woman will meet those standards without us having to lower them. Wait on the **LORD**! We don't know what's best for us; only *GOD* does—so, why not wait? I want everything God has for me and nothing of what I think is best for me.

Today, I am a single woman, and it feels **GREAT**! I can focus more on God and myself. I can continue to grow and become the best Proverbs 31 Woman I can be while preparing myself for when God does send Mr. Right.

The lesson here is this: We must learn to stop asking God for "just someone" while we're lonely. Be **SPECIFIC**. Know that God answers prayers, so (I repeat) be *SPECIFIC*! If only I would've paid attention early on in that relationship, I wouldn't have endured 18 months of toxicity. Believe it or not, I am grateful for the experience and the lesson. I suffered sorrow, pain, and shed a lot of tears, but God kept me. There were times I wanted to give up, but God kept me. Everything in our life happens for a reason. Everyone who comes into your life is there for a reason.

As for me, when I finally released all those toxic feelings, I became **FREE**! Oh, my! The **JOY** I felt of knowing God kept me! The **JOY** I felt when my mind was cleared of the fog! The **JOY** I felt when I began to have an even closer walk with God! The **JOY** I felt when I could love me more than ever!

I shed no more tears of sadness. All my tears are full of **JOY**! To the Lord, I say, *"Thank You! You are worthy to be praised!"*

To you, I say, *"Be **FREE**! Wait on God! Be patient! And, most importantly, love yourself first!"*

Compiled by Angela R. Edwards

Keywana Wright

Dedication:
I thank God for this opportunity to share my testimony with you. I pray you will be inspired. Be true to yourself. Never let others steal your **JOY!**

Bio:
Keywana Wright is a native of Flint, Michigan, and devoted mother of one daughter, Tayler Wright-Williams. She is an Author, Life Coach, Prayer Warrior, Speaker, and Director of "Proverbs 31 Woman Empowerment Session." She has a God-given love for women, helping them reach their purpose in the Kingdom of God, and is a believer in the power of prayer. Her favorite Bible verse is, *"In all thy ways, acknowledge Him and He shall direct thy path"* (Proverbs 3:6). Keywana holds a Bachelor of Arts in Family Life Education from Spring Arbor University and a certificate in Leadership in Ministry from New Creation School of Leadership in Flint, Michigan.

Finding the Joy After the Pain

"These things I have spoken to you so that My joy may be in you, and that your joy may be made full" (John 15:11).

Have you ever told someone you love them? I have. I've even uttered the words, *"Girl, I found the man of my dreams!"*

Have you ever said to yourself, *"This is Mr./Mrs. Right!"* — only to have the love you once felt turn into pain? Yes, love can cause pain… "growing pains."

Take a walk with me down Memory Lane as I tried to bounce back from failed relationships to finding joy after the pain. I ran from relationship to relationship, looking for joy. At the time, I didn't acknowledge that **TRUE JOY** only comes from the Lord.

I grew up in Flint, Michigan — a city where you may have heard about the water crisis in April of 2014. I was raised in a two-parent home, where my father was the breadwinner. My mother worked part-time outside of the home, but her main focus was on raising my two older brothers (one of them passed away due to gun violence in 2002) and me. My parents divorced when I was 16 years old. Although I grew up with both of my parents in the home, I still struggled with maintaining healthy relationships.

My relationship struggles started when I was in high school. I met my high school sweetheart at the age of 16 — around the same time my parents separated. "Puppy Love" is what it was called, but I thought I was in *LOVE*. My hormones were out of control. I was that teenager who was looking for love in all the wrong places. My first love was also my first boyfriend. For the next 16 years, we dated on and off.

After high school, I attended Mott College and obtained an Associate's Degree in Arts, all while working two jobs and maintaining my one-bedroom apartment. After graduating, I then transferred to Spring Arbor University and obtained a Bachelor's Degree in Family Life Education. In the interim, I worked various jobs as a Daycare Worker, Respite Worker, and later, at a local women's shelter. Finally, I landed a career position at the Department of Health and Human Services. I was living my best life! I even had a man who "completed" me. I was so happy with where I was in life…at least that's what I thought.

I had no clue at the time that love could hurt. I was a Christian and professed Jesus Christ as Lord. I attended church regularly, sang in the choir, and was on the praise team. Yes, I was a church girl with an issue: I had a relationship with God but wrestled with not committing fornication. As much as I tried to live a holy lifestyle, the fight with sexual sin was a problem. I even prayed and asked God to help me and, for a period, was doing fine. I thought I was delivered…until my ex-boyfriend came around from time to time. Then, I would find myself back in sexual sin's stronghold.

The time came when I could no longer hide my sin from others. In 2009, I became pregnant with my daughter. I can clearly recall the day I told my daughter's father. He walked into my bedroom and sat on the bed. I was both nervous and excited at the same time. I shared with him what I **thought** would be exciting news:

"I am pregnant."

He stared at me for what seemed like hours. Finally, he uttered the words, *"I am not ready to be a father."* Immediately after speaking those heart-wrenching words, he walked out…never to be seen or heard from again.

I was **HURT**! I trusted him. Never in a *million years* would I have guessed he would just walk away as if I were a stranger off the street. At the time, I felt like one of those "Call Girls." I was 32 years old, pregnant, and soon to be a single parent.

The following week, I told my pastor about my "situation." Because of the shame I felt, I thought it was best to stop participating in my ministries. No longer did I want to sing in the choir or praise team. I didn't want others to think it was okay to have a child out of wedlock. However, my pastor wouldn't let me walk away. I recall him praying for me and then saying, *"Don't worry; be happy. Everything will be okay."* I remember crying and accepting what he said. My church family was also very supportive. They embraced me, which I believe was God's way of showing that He loved me and forgave me for my sins. My pain was turning into joy again. I was learning true joy comes from God. Scripture states, *"The joy of the Lord is my strength"* (Nehemiah 8:10).

I want to pause my story here and encourage you at this moment. Know that God is **always** there, even amid your mess. He *wants* you to cry out to Him for help and repentance. He loves you and wants the best for you. Just as my pastor told me,

I sow the following words into your spirit-woman/spirit-man: **Don't worry; be happy!** God wants you to trust Him and not worry. He desires that you give Him **every** issue or situation in which you find yourself. He can deliver you from them all. He wants you to be happy and content in Him. **GOD IS JOY!**

So, my life got back on track, and I enjoyed being pregnant. While with child in my womb, I met another man online. He lived in another state, and we talked on the phone and facetimed each other often. He worked on the oil rig ships offshore, which gave him plenty of time to talk to me when he wasn't busy. We kept each other company and enjoyed every conversation. He was a gentleman and kind. After about a month, he requested to visit me in person. I quickly agreed to the visit. I was about 2 ½ months pregnant at the time but had yet to tell him because I wanted to do so face-to-face. Once he arrived, we went out to dinner. It was then I told him I was pregnant. We talked for hours that night about my child's father and the situation I was in. He concluded our conversation by stating we would remain friends. After all, no one really knew at that time what the outcome of our relationship would be.

As my story continues, I married the man who promised to be my friend. My daughter was almost three years old when we exchanged our vows. I had found joy through pain, rejection, and shame! I had been made whole. My life was complete. My daughter finally had a father—a man she could call "daddy." My dream had come true!

That was until the honeymoon period came to an end…

Even though I had a great support system of family and friends, things happened in my life that hit me so hard, I was temporarily robbed of my **joy**.

That year, I had my fair share of happiness **and** disappointments. Reality set in, and major decisions had to be made. I learned my daughter had Attention Deficit Hyperactivity Disorder (commonly known as ADHD). My husband was very supportive. When he was off from work, we managed to go to family therapy and doctor's appointments together. He was still working offshore in Louisiana, often out of reach for 60 days at a time. I was accustomed to his absence because while dating, we were miles apart from one another.

However, over a period of time, being apart started weighing heavily on our marriage. The happiness I once felt turned into pain again. At that point in my life, I had developed a closer relationship with God, so I prayed and gave our marriage to Him.

Soon enough, we had yet another decision to make: Which one of us would relocate? I resided in Michigan, and he lived in Texas. Neither one of us wanted to relocate for various reasons. In the end, we chose to continue living apart and travel to see each other often. As time progressed, our separation had taken its toll on our marriage. Eventually, we separated and then divorced.

I truly had to rely on God for strength. I had experienced yet another love story that turned into pain. I remember the days when I would question myself. ***"What is wrong with me? Why does it seem that when I find love, it turns into pain?"*** One day, while praying to God, I heard Him say, *"Man will fail* *you; I never will. I will give you peace that will surpass all your understanding. I will give you joy in the midst of your sorrow. Trust Me: I have a plan for your life. Everything will work out."* When I gave **ALL** my pain to God, He restored my joy!

At the time of this writing, I am engaged to another man. This time, I've decided to take my time — **AND** date someone who *at least* lives in the same state. I can say I have now found **TRUE JOY** that only comes from God. It was important for me to realize that my joy comes from God and Him alone. I was able to find joy after the pain.

I want to encourage you by letting you know this: No matter what you go through in life, God is always there with you — especially in those moments when you think He is not. He will **NEVER** leave nor forsake you. He loves you, and His love is everlasting and unconditional. He **WILL** turn your pain into joy!

Cindy H. Reed

Dedication:
I dedicate this writing to my mother, Ellen Hillery.
Mom, you're an amazing mother, person, and friend.
I thank God for you. Thank you for loving me.

Bio:
Cindy H. Reed was born and raised in New York. She's published in Diamonds and Pearls – 1997, Best Poems of 1998, and Timeless Voices – 2006. In 2014, she was a featured reader of one of her writings at the "FCAC Literary Expo" in Washington, DC. In 2016, Cindy published her first book titled *Twisted Reality*. In 2018, Cindy was a featured Fashion Designer for her Creations by Cindy's Hands jewelry line, in York County Fashion Week. Cindy's jewelry is sold in two retail stores: Charlotte, NC and Fort Mill, SC. In 2019, Cindy published her second book titled *Diesel: The Dittleberry's Diva*.

Compiled by Angela R. Edwards

My Journey — God's Delivery

Lord, let my transparency reach the depths of my soul, allowing my story to bring You glory and encourage others.

2017: Mother's Day weekend. I drove my rental truck down Interstate 95 with my Volkswagen Beetle hitched to the back. Five days earlier, I'd decided that I needed to leave my very toxic marriage. I had no plan; I just needed out—**quick!** My sanity depended on it.

After relocating to my mother's home, I immediately began my search for a job. I looked for work **everywhere**. My 36 years of Admin experience nor my 20-year career with a major corporation was helping me land a job. I either made too much money in the past, or my tenure with that huge corporation turned into, *"Why would you want to work for us?"* I knew I wanted a different career for the second part of my life; I just didn't know what that would look like. I also knew I had a lot to offer but needed someone to see that in me. In the meantime, I worked temp assignments.

2018: What? Did I just hear what I thought I heard? I quickly made my way to the television to hear about an actress who had breast cancer and was going through treatments.

I asked myself, *"When was the last time you did a self-exam?"* I then lifted my arms and began my self-check. **"What the heck?! Oh no, it's not! It can't be! Is that a lump?!"**

Home alone for the entire weekend, I had to wait until Monday morning to be seen at Urgent Care. I didn't want panic and fear to set in, so I immediately went to the Lord in prayer. I asked God to keep me calm and not to let my finding be cancer. After praying, I called my mom to share with her.

As it turned out, the nurse didn't find anything. She recommended that I have a mammogram, just to be sure. The mammogram didn't show anything in my left breast (where I felt something), but it did, however, show a mass in my right breast. I had to have a biopsy done and, while I was at work, my doctor called me with the results. He stated I had breast cancer and that we needed to schedule surgery right away.

I'm not sure I can articulate the realness of the fog I was in after hearing those words…

Since I was at work, I couldn't talk about it with anyone. I couldn't think clearly, so I texted everyone in my immediate family:

"I have breast cancer. Surgery is needed right away."

Perhaps it wasn't the *best* decision to text, but I couldn't talk on the phone, and I needed my family to know so they could start praying for me.

After meeting with my surgeon in August 2018, I found out I had Carcinoma in Situ. My surgeon told me it wasn't breast cancer, but without the surgery to remove it, it would develop into breast cancer. I was Stage Zero. **#Blessed**

I fired my Primary Care doctor—the one who called and told me I had breast cancer—and filed a complaint against him.

My surgery was scheduled for the following month (September). All turned out well. **#Blessed**

Three days after my surgery, I interviewed for a full-time administrative position. I landed the job and started work on October 1st. Later that month, my mom told me she was selling her house and that there was no rush for me to move. Needless to say, her home sold quickly. We all needed to be out in January.

At the time, my life seemed to be spiraling out of control. Nothing was happening the way I wanted it to, leaving me feeling overwhelmed.

- A broken marriage
- Starting my life over
- Not finding a good job
- Being in the breast cancer family
- Mom relocating

I started shutting down slowly and quietly.

In November, I began looking at apartments. I knew I needed some sense of stability. I wanted to remain living in the part of town I was familiar with, so I found an apartment five minutes from my mom's house. Two days before I was to move in, I did my walkthrough. The apartment I was shown wasn't like the one I'd initially viewed. It was old, dark, not updated, etc. I complained to no end. I wasn't happy at all. I took pictures of everything I found wrong with the place. They knew they'd messed up with me, but I was stuck. There was no time to do anything different. I walked away from that meeting feeling broken.

The next day, the rental office called to tell me they had another more updated apartment available for me — **better** than the one I'd initially seen and liked. The only concern was that they had to clean and prepare it for me, and I wouldn't be able to see it before my move-in date…which was the following day. I told them, *"YES! I'll take it!"* It was everything they described to me, and I was happy to call that new place "HOME." I couldn't stop thanking God for that blessing. On December 1st, I moved in. **#AnchoredInFaith**

For the entire month of December, my mom remained in her home. She wanted to have one last Christmas there with her children and grandchildren. One day after work, just as I pulled into my parking space, my mom called. She wanted to know where I was, if I was still coming over for dinner, and when I would get there. I knew something was up. I asked her if everything was okay. She said she needed to talk to me, but she wouldn't tell me anything over the phone. Since I heard the urgency in her voice, I didn't get out of my car. Instead, I just backed up and headed to her house.

Once there, my mom told me the doctors believed she had Stage 4 Lung Cancer. My heart sank. I listened to her, trying to be strong and not cry, but I was crushed on the inside. Nothing at the time was confirmed, so I pulled strength from that. I managed to give her some comforting words and could see that my strength got her through that moment. **#ILoveMyMommy**

In January 2019, my mom's diagnosis was confirmed. I believe that's the darkest thing I've ever had to deal with in my life. Watching her go through the process of asking questions, dealing with emotions, etc., was more emotional for me than hearing I had breast cancer. I couldn't make it any better for her. I couldn't take it away. I couldn't be there for her like I wanted to because, in January, she relocated to another city. I was all alone with no family around.

With all I'd gone through since relocating, I began to fall into a deep depression. I began crying at everything — stuff that didn't make any sense to cry over. I didn't want to be around anyone or talk to anyone on the phone. I never left the house except to go to work. I stopped creating jewelry. I stopped keeping my house organized. I found myself looking forward to 5:00 p.m. because once I was in my car, I didn't have to talk to anyone again until the next day. I dove deeper and deeper into depression and couldn't pull myself out.

****

I had an appointment to meet with my Oncologist, who told me I had to take a pill once a day — for five years — to help prevent me from getting breast cancer. One side effect of the medicine is severe hot flashes. He assured me they would eventually subside. Having already experienced hot flashes, I wasn't happy about that news but knew there was nothing I could do about it. While speaking with my doctor, I began to cry. At that time in my life, I cried about any and everything, and hearing that I had to take a pill for the next five years to help prevent me from getting breast cancer (with the possibility I could still get it), well, it didn't take much for the tears to flow.

At that moment, I knew I needed to confide in my doctor. I asked him if he could give me some medicine to help with my depression. To my surprise, he told me there was a medication that would help with the hot flashes and was known to help with depression. He wanted me to build up my system with the hot flash control medicine for three months before starting my one-pill-a-day cancer prevention medicine.

Initially, as I took the hot flash control medicine, I started feeling a little better, but that didn't last long. When I thought things couldn't get any worse, they did. In May 2019, I lost my job. The company took good care of me financially for a month and provided me with a great Letter of Recommendation. They also approved me for unemployment. All that was a blessing in a *"Why is this happening to me?"* time in my life.

As I continued taking the medication, I began smelling it come through my skin. On top of everything else going on, I felt I smelled strange. It wasn't constant, but it was often enough that I knew it was the medicine—yet I continued taking it and never mentioned the symptom to my doctor. As I look back on it now, I realize I just wasn't in my right mind. But God continued to keep me when I didn't know I was being kept!

I believe the medicine was working against me and not for me, yet I continued taking it. Then, one day, I heard the voice of the Lord say, *"Cindy, stop taking that medicine!"* I knew it was God. I obeyed and immediately threw out the pills. As the days passed, I began to feel different…better! The Cindy I knew was emerging. I'd found my smile again. God healed me, and I was on the road to recovery! **#Blessed**

I was only out of work for two months, working temp assignments here and there, when I landed a job in a new career field. Finally! What I wanted people to do, they were doing: looking at my skills and knowing I'd be perfect for the position. I couldn't stop thanking God for not only saving me from myself but for blessing me with a new job on a totally new career path. Since July 1, 2019, I've been in the position of Marketing and Exhibits Coordinator for a publishing company! How ironic is it that my being an author and having published two books, I am now learning the inner workings of a publishing company?!

I thanked God for that Heaven-sent blessing of a new job/new career—and it came with having my own, large office. As an Admin, I'd never had an office. God is good! I remained faithful through every teardrop, every prayer. My mom has been doing well ever since her diagnosis. To look at her, you'd never know she's dealing with Stage 4 Lung Cancer, but to God we give the glory. She is living her best life! The cancer hasn't spread, and she's very happy in her new house. Her blessing is a shared blessing because if she's happy, I can't ask for more.

If you're going through anything negative in life, continue to have faith and hold on to God's unchanging hands because He will be there for you. He will bring you out. Just remain faithful and know He's got you. **There is no situation bigger than our God!**

Clarence Jordan, Jr.

Dedication:
In memoriam of my late father, Pastor Clarence Jordan, Sr. He would be well-pleased with me as an accomplished author.

Bio:
Clarence Jordan, Jr. is an International Best-Selling Author of the book *Blessed Trinity: God the Father, God the Son, God the Holy Ghost*. He is a resident of Minneapolis, Minnesota, where he graduated from South High School in 1985. In August 2000, Clarence was ordained as an Elder under the Church of God in Christ.

Compiled by Angela R. Edwards

My God, My Protector

Following are my personal testimonies of victory—times when divine intervention supernaturally caused miracles to happen in my life. My stories provide evidence that God will **always** protect His children from hurt, harm, and danger. I'm delighted to share with you and pray you are encouraged as you reflect on times when God interceded on your behalf.

One particular morning, I had a very vivid dream. In the vision, I saw a demon that was masquerading as a man. He stood tall and erect as if he was a soldier in the Army. His eyes were the most memorable aspect of his physique. They were light blue and transfixed on me. If looks could kill, he could have certainly done so without the use of a weapon. The demon's clothing was unique, as well. He wore a Texas Ranger-style hat with a wide brim (similar to that of those worn by the police force) and a long, dark khaki-colored trench coat. There was no appearance of a background scene, just pitch-black darkness that enveloped him.

About 3:20 a.m., I **immediately** awoke from my sleep. My spirit-man was disturbed by that unusual and uncanny dream. At that moment, I felt a mix of emotions to include fear, thinking perhaps the vision was a foreshadowing of someone contemplating breaking into my house. I got out of bed and knelt at my bedside to pray. After praying, I was convinced by the Holy Spirit that God would protect me from *whatever* danger lurked ahead. After giving God praise in advance for what He was about to do, I climbed back into bed and fell fast asleep.

God's Joy Fruit

Later on, around 5:00 that morning, I awoke and prepared for my workday. At the time, I had no vehicle, so I had to leave a little earlier than usual to catch the city bus. I recall it being unusually dark as I made my way to the bus stop on foot—a walk that took about 45 minutes from my home. At roughly 6:15 a.m., I was just about midway to my destination when suddenly, I noticed a man coming out of a dark area where one would normally self-wash their car. Much like in my dream, he was staring at me and slowly easing his way toward me. He had no weapon in his hands, but I could *FEEL* his intentions were **pure evil**.

All the while, I remained watchful and prayerful…

There were bushes that separated the parking lot of the self-service car wash from the sidewalk on which I walked. I believe his goal was to attack me from behind. Once he cleared the bushes, without hesitation, I turned to my left and faced him. In that brief moment, I observed his eyes. They were **identical** to what I had envisioned in my dream! He immediately turned and ran away from me.

Later that day, I realized God was letting me know that the attacker was unable to get anywhere near me because **GOD** had intervened on my behalf as my *PROTECTOR!*

****

Compiled by Angela R. Edwards

My Guardian Angel at Work

One early morning in February 2016, the alarm clock buzzer sounded around 5:00 a.m., alerting me to awake from my sleep. Immediately, I got out of bed and began to prepare for the workday ahead. As I left out of my house, I made sure I had locked the door behind me and then double-checked to make sure it was secured.

I remember it being dark and cold that morning. At the time, I was without a vehicle, so I had to travel on foot from my home to the city bus stop—a walk that took me approximately 45 minutes one way. While walking, I was continually watching and praying against any imminent danger *(we never know where danger is lurking)*. Just as I made it to the corner and turned right, I noticed a medium-sized black and brown dog. It was unrestrained, standing on the grass near the corner house, and staring at me. Since the dog did not bark or show any signs of aggression toward me, I kept on walking.

I then noticed another unrestrained medium-sized tan-colored dog. It was heading towards me from the opposite end of the block. It was clear to me both dogs had their eyes fixed on each other. The tan dog then ran up to the black and brown one, and they began playing with each other on the grass for a moment. In the blink of an eye, all of that changed. Both dogs quickly focused their attention directly on me. I became their **prime target**.

Both then began running towards me. Their aggressive nature could not be mistaken: I was sure to be attacked by those hounds—*or was I?*

God's Joy Fruit

As they came closer, the Holy Spirit instructed me to walk courageously toward them. Yes, you read that correctly. I was told to walk **directly** into the face of adversity. I remained calm, even though the snarling dogs were drawing closer and closer to me. I just **KNEW** God would protect me from harm! Suddenly, their all-out sprint came to a complete stop—as if they had simultaneously stepped on the brakes. After a brief pause, both looked up toward the sky, obviously sensing another, *more powerful* presence. Fear gripped them, and, with a frightened yelp, they immediately took off running in a tremendous hurry to get away from me.

The last I saw them, they were cowered in a dark area of the neighborhood, hiding from my guardian angel—the one **GOD** had sent to protect me.

I experienced great **JOY** and peace, knowing my Heavenly Father always watched over me.

Marvell Gales

Dedication:

To my Lord and Savior Jesus Christ: I am nothing without You and everything with You! To my Dad: I'm humbly grateful and blessed to have you in my life.

Bio:

Marvell Gales is a woman after God's own heart. She is a Certified Life Coach, Certified Christian Counselor, and Intercessor in the Kingdom of God. She published two Best-Selling books: *INNER ME* and *Motherless Daughter*. Recently, she launched "Majestic Godly Ministries Foundation, Inc." — a foundation geared to inspire, encourage, and empower women. Marvell states, *"I have a plethora of accolades, awards, and accomplishments; however, the one thing that matters the most is my true and sincere relationship with the Lord and Savior Jesus Christ."*

JOY'S Perfect Place

For I now **KNOW** that the true **"JOY"** of the Lord is my strength! I can now dwell in this perfect place forevermore, simply because the joy I now possess comes from my Lord and Savior Jesus Christ. At the mention of the name of the Lord, I exhale with a deep sigh, knowing who I am truly am in Christ Jesus. Mere words cannot express or explain this feeling; it is simply exhilarating, to say the least.

When I was younger, I used to be afraid to make mention of being physically abused by the one person who gave me life. Unfortunately, she was the one we are supposed to call "momma." I did not have the greatest experience as a child. Growing up, I did not know why I was the one who was the "black sheep," if you will. As I grew older and wiser, I learned within my most inner-self that God had His *HANDS* on me all my life—the entire time.

"What is JOY?" they ask.

"A happy place!" is how they would always respond.

A **HAPPY** place? *Hmm...* As I pondered where that place is and what it looks like, I would wander aimlessly, seeking the "happy place" that everyone was talking about. I desperately desired it, longed for it, and actually went in search of it. Oh, that journey was full of ups and downs, with lots of mixed emotions and feelings I could not explain.

Talk about an emotional roller coaster! Yes, it was! Some days, it was cool and even fun. Then, there were days when I felt as if I wanted to get hit by a train. The painful feelings would hurt so badly. There would be days when I'd sit and think to myself (and even express aloud), *"Is this really **JOY**? Is it supposed to feel this way?"* The asking of those questions made me wonder all the more about how dreadful my childhood life truly was, especially if I had to ask myself those questions.

"Hey, girl! What's up?"

"Ah, nothing much."

"Why do you sound so down?"

"This is my normal sound...remember?"

"Umm, yep. But can you cheer up a bit?"

"What do I need to cheer up about? This is my old, boring life. Nothing in it is exciting, so I don't need to be happy about anything!"

"Girl, we are coming to get you out of that house. Get dressed because we're on our way!"

(Ten minutes later, there's a honk of a horn. I run out the front door and into the four-door sedan.)

"You ready to have some fun?"

"What kind of fun?"

"You'll see. Just wait!"

"What's this shack house? I'm not going in there!"

"Girl, come on. These are the livest parties ever! Just come on!"

"Naw, I'm not going in there. It looks scary, and the people look cracked out to me!"

"You won't have to worry about them. They aren't even at the party. They are just passing by, looking for some change."

"Yep. Whatever. I'm not going to be here long, so get ready to take me home soon!"

(Two hours later, we were still kicking it with the 'hood folks.')

The ride home that night was exciting. I suppose we talked about **everything** that went on at the party—from the food to the cool people I met. The DJ played some great music on the turntables, which led to me meeting a nice guy. The party itself was nothing to actually brag about to others because a lot of people wouldn't understand the hood's logic. Even for me, it took me some time to learn precisely what it was and who the people are in it. For some odd reason, I always thought "hood folks" would be the worse people on the planet, but they turned out to be cool to me. Although some were a tad bit obnoxious and 'untamed' (if you will), many were down to earth and really cool people—well, at least to me.

The guy I met at the party that night was charming, handsome, and very sweet to me. His smile was to die for, and he had dimples for days! I liked him a lot. We talked and talked for days…weeks…and months. It was refreshing to speak to him. Daily, I awaited his phone call.

I would also anticipate going on dates with him. It was amazing to feel that way and to even be in that place. At that moment, I believed I had found my "happy place"—that **JOY** that everyone talked about. Yes, I found **JOY** with him.

For months, he never skipped a beat. He was very consistent and reliable, always making sure I was okay. He kept a smile on my face. I knew at that point I had arrived at where everyone else was. Those 14 months were the best ever for me...*at least that's what I thought.*

One day, he called to tell me he was relocating to another state because he had gotten a job promotion. My heart immediately sank. I was left breathless. I thought I was going to die. I fell silent on my end of the line for at least two to three minutes. He kept saying, *"Hello? Hello?"* but I was left both horrified and speechless. After finding my voice again, I asked him the one question that I was afraid of him to answer:

"What about us? What about **ME**?"

He politely stated, *"We will be no more. I gotta go and make my money."*

I hung up the phone in his face and never looked back. It was at that very moment when I began to seek and search for my Creator...the One who created me in His own image...the One who is the Author and Finisher of my faith: **GOD**.

After days on top of days seeking the Lord our God, I finally **FOUND** Him! Now, granted, I was in a very dark place when I discovered Him, it was the most perfect place I needed to be at that particular time. I began to read the Word of God, all while asking Him for an understanding of what it was that I was reading. I will admit that when I started to read the Word of God, I got overwhelmed with so much of what was contained therein. There was a lot of which I was totally unaware.

God's Joy Fruit

Growing up, going to church was a must. If I were to be honest, we went because we had no other choice. If someone would have asked us, *"What are you going to church for?"* or *"What are you learning at church?"*, I promise you this: We would **NOT** have been able to tell them. Unfortunately, we were not taught about church, God, and their *significance*. It makes sense to me now why the Bible teaches us to seek the Lord for ourselves and study to shew thyself approved unto God, a workman that needeth not be ashamed, rightly dividing the Word of Truth (2 Timothy 2:15).

I vividly remember reading the Books of the Bible by chapters. I started with John and then moved on to Esther, Jeremiah, 1st and 2nd Corinthians, and finishing with Galatians. Galatians was a fascinating Book of the Bible. Many of its chapters were "ah-ha moments" for me. That was when I actually learned that the word **'JOY'** was a Fruit of the Holy Spirit! I later learned that the **JOY** we possess comes from the Lord. Galatians 5:22-23 explains the Fruit of the Spirit and how each should be shown and displayed to others here on earth as it is in Heaven. That was, indeed, good news to me!

I'm constantly reminded of Psalm 28:7 that says, *"My heart leaps with JOY, and I will give thanks to Him in song."* That passage makes sense to me now because ever since I sought the Lord and found Him, there has been a song in my heart that gleams with so much **JOY**—an unspeakable **JOY** that is relatively hard to express or explain. Nonetheless, knowing that confirms the following: No matter who I meet or how much I love someone, I cannot allow them to validate or dictate my **JOY**! They didn't give it to me (because they do not have the capacity to do so); therefore, they *CANNOT* take it away.

God is **POWERFUL**. He gives us all of what we need in His Kingdom to be able to exemplify who He really is on earth as He is in Heaven.

I used to think I was content with those things I associated with happiness and joy coming from an individual until the following two factors were illuminated in my life:

1. Knowing precisely what **JOY** is; and
2. Realizing that true **JOY** comes from the Lord and permeates from the inside out.

An individual who is truly in Christ Jesus will experience the full extent of what **JOY** is and how it exudes and radiates into the atmosphere. Many people do not experience the true essence of **JOY**, mainly because they aren't aware of **JOY's** true meaning.

Webster's Dictionary defines joy as *"the emotion evoked by well-being, success, or good fortune or by the prospect of possessing what one desires."* The *world* tends to think that definition is the true essence of **JOY**; however, in the spiritual realm, **JOY** is described in the following manner:

"These things have I spoken unto you, that My joy might remain in you, and that your joy might be full" (John 15:11).

"Seek ye first the Kingdom of God and all of His righteousness, and all these things will be added unto you" (Matthew 6:33).

"Joy is the settled assurance that God is in control of all the details of my life, the quiet confidence that ultimately, everything is going to be alright, and the determined choice to praise God in every situation" (Warren, 2012).

PRAYER

Father God, thy good and faithful King and Ruler of all things on earth and in Heaven:

We submit and surrender unto Your authority right now. We thank You for being God. We need You and cannot make it on earth without You. As we go through our days on earth, some come to You for one thing, and others go to You for something else. Even in that, we still say thank You, Lord God.

Lord, as we continue to seek you and humble ourselves before You, we ask that you continue to have mercy on our lives, Lord. Continue to grant Your mercy and grace to us, Lord. Saturate our minds and hearts with nothing but things that are from above, things that are holy, things that are righteous, and things that are simply of You, Lord God. Teach us how to walk and talk like You. Teach us how to *LOVE* like You, Master. Rain down on us that **JOY**, unspeakable **JOY** that only comes from You! We need it like never before, God.

When this life is over here on earth, we'll be careful to give Your name the glory, honor, praise, and worship that is due unto You, Father God.

This is my prayer for Your people, Lord God, in Jesus' name.

Amen and Amen.

Compiled by Angela R. Edwards

Nikki Denise

Dedication:

First, I give honor to God for being the head of my life. Thank you to the following women for their support: Natasha Banister, Micheline Barber, Marsha Baldwin, Laticia Nicole, Velma Greenlee, and Terry Spicer.

Bio:

Nikki Denise is a Licensed Cosmetologist, Educator, Author, Certified Skin Care Specialist, and is known as "The Social Butterfly" on social media platforms. Her literary pursuits to date include her first book titled "Overcomer," where she shares her personal testimony, and co-author of "The Purposed Woman: 365 Days Devotional" (2019), "I Was Her" (2020), "The Principal of the Beauty CEO" (2020), and "God's Joy Fruit" (2020). Nikki is the Founder and CEO of her beauty company, N Denise Intraprises, LLC, where she educates others about proper skincare while providing support and encouragement.

For Chrissakes: I Was Just a Child!

At the age of 14, I was forced to learn what being an adult was like. I had no idea how to care for a family. After all, the adults should have been taking care of **ME**! I was the one who needed looking after. Discovering what life was all about at that tender age was something I was not at all prepared for, yet life has a way of dealing a bad hand sometimes.

Being raped by a family member was the most devastating moment in my life. Being hushed into silence was all the more devastating. My rapist told me, *"I will kill you if you tell anyone."* The silence was my bedfellow.

My sorrows didn't stop there.

My father passed away, and my mother found comfort at the other end of a bottle as she mourned the loss of a child. My environment was toxic and one no child should ever have to experience. Watching my mother sick with alcoholism was difficult, so much so to the point that on my 15th birthday, I informed her I was leaving home at the age of 16 and would never return. She looked at me with fault in her eyes and said, *"Whatever. I don't believe you will make it out there."* That was just the fuel I needed. I left home when I said I would, and, at the age of 17, my mother couldn't help but acknowledge my determination. She said, **"Well, you made a liar out of me!"**

My grandma was my backbone. As I write this, tears are falling because I remember the times my grandma prayed for me. I recall the lessons of a praying grandmother. I knew then, and I know now that those prayers will carry me all the days of my life. In time, I discovered God and how to pray for myself. That was an invaluable lesson at the time. I was a high school dropout who was maintaining responsibility for myself, bills, and all other things. Because of the rape and continual buildup of pains associated with that tragic event, I felt as if I had to stay busy to rebuild my self-esteem. I also began attending therapy sessions to help deal with those past pains.

Sadly, at the age of 18, I lost my first child. That loss broke me all the way down to what I believed to be a point of no return. Still today, I often wonder what it would have been like to have an older sibling for my child. Only God knows best, though! After the loss of my first child, I remember thinking, *"I am **NEVER** going to have children!"*

NEVER tell the **LORD** what you're **NOT** going to do!

At the age of 28, I was raped again. What pulled up and out of those volcanic eruptions? Prayer, fasting, and the strength that **ONLY** God could provide.

Today, I am a single mother of my son, Jai'saiah…and I am truly thankful for him.

I want to encourage you today by letting you know you, too, can overcome your problems, trials, and tests. The way you do that is by surrendering yourself to your God in Heaven — not yourself nor anyone else. Focus on the next day…and then the next. If necessary, go to therapy to get assistance with the healing process. Forgiveness for yourself is required, as well. Always know that God loves you.

Stay the course, and never give up. I didn't, and today, I'm 40 years old. I can tell you that everything I endured is a part of my journey. Heck yeah, I was mad at God for a time because I couldn't understand why He allowed someone to cause me harm. When I tell you God brought forth suffering to those who hurt me, He did just that. Walk your walk in life, knowing that God has His hands on everything, everyone, and every part of your life. Your journey is unique, so take comfort in knowing that whatever your purpose is in life, God's timing is always perfect. He will never leave you and will provide a way out of no way.

I am honored to share my testimony with you and pray that all things will work together for the good of those who are called by His name. Always know the **KING OF KINGS** is in you! Be blessed, and may God keep you always and forevermore!

In closing, I leave the following three passages of scripture with you:

Matthew 9:16 - *"No one sews a patch of unshrunk cloth on an old garment, for the patch will pull away from the garment, making the tear worse."*

John 3:16 - *"For God so loved the world that he gave his one and only Son, that whoever believes in him shall not perish but have eternal life."*

2 Corinthians 4:16 - *"Therefore we do not lose heart. Though outwardly, we are wasting away, yet inwardly we are being renewed day by day. For our light and momentary."*

Compiled by Angela R. Edwards

Shanericka Jones

"…and those the LORD has rescued will return. They will enter Zion with singing; everlasting joy will crown their heads. Gladness and joy will overtake them, and sorrow and sighing will flee away."

Isaiah 35:10

Joy the World Didn't Give

For a great deal of my life, I lived selfishly. Admittedly, I acted very spoiled *(dare I say "bratty"?)*. My actions and attitude caused me to hurt a lot of people during those times, whether it be by words or actions.

Growing up, I thought **"JOY"** was getting the latest clothes, hanging with my friends, and just having a constant good time. I both sought and yearned for those "things." My mom did her best to fill our home with happiness and ensured that we lacked nothing.

Around the time middle school age came, my life became awkward. Before I knew it, I floated around here and there, trying to find someplace — **ANY** place — to fit in. From 6th grade to 12th, I merely existed …literally. After graduating high school, I thought I was grown and married who I believed was to be my forever love. Tragically, his life was taken suddenly, sending me into a downward spiral seemingly overnight.

I was bombarded with "advice." People *(who likely meant well)* told me how I should feel and how fast I should go through my grieving process. Their "advice" only served to send me deeper into a self-induced hell. During the process, I can say I had virtually no real sense of happiness, let alone even know what the word **"JOY"** meant or what place it had in my life. After my husband's death, I incorporated fillers *(better known as 'distractions')*. Those distractions drew me further and further away from God, my family, and even myself because I began to feel completely alone. The search for **"JOY"** was continual.

I did all kinds of things to fill the void to include getting high to self-medicate my self-pity. At one point, I turned to prostitution to help feed the addiction I created during those times of depression. I was walking in the ultimate state of denial. As a result, while I was still going to school, I ended up failing the classes that would have propelled me into my career choice. For a while, I was working and collecting Social Security. In 2012, I stopped working and was granted full Social Security Disability benefits due to depression and relapse on PCP *(commonly known as 'Angel Dust')* that almost extinguished my life.

Then came another time when things started to spin out of control just when life appeared to be pieced altogether. For instance, I once found myself driving down a major highway one day heading to my husband's gravesite. Along the way, I was getting high and soon blacked out. I came out of my drug-induced stupor in the middle of the freeway to a firetruck behind me and a fireman at my window asking me if everything was okay.

I thank God for His protection, covering, and angels He sent to keep me during those stormy times in my life.

In 2015, I was finally permitted to be in a setting where I was sat down in a place where I had nothing but time to think and do a self-evaluation. As well, I was afforded the opportunity to seek God in a way I had never done before. True **"JOY"** came when I embraced the solid foundation built on God's Word and looked towards Jesus. The incessant fog of depression lifted, and I finally felt **FREE!** *(This happened at a time in my life when I had left all my family and had no choice but to focus on me and what needed to be done to help me be a "better **ME**.")*

As life would have it, in 2016, my mom's health began to deteriorate, requiring around-the-clock help with things we often take for granted, such as eating and going to the restroom alone. When the time came that she needed a caregiver, I was able to work part-time to take care of her — which brought me a form of **"JOY"** you cannot even begin to imagine. To finally be in a place in life where I was not looked at as "a mess-up," all while being able to help someone who loved me *(even at my worst)* was a wonderful feeling! It was the first time I didn't expect "what I could get out of this" because I was reminded of **ALL** that I gained:

- I spent quality time with my mom.
- I cared for the same woman who nursed me back to life when I failed at a suicide attempt.
- I catered to the same one who helped me with my baby when I couldn't even help myself.

To know I helped my mom without expectation of anything in return *(other than ensuring she was comfortable and had no worries)* helped me through those tough times. When the moment came and she passed away, I was able to still hold on to the **"JOY"** of the Lord because I have the faith that she is with our Savior and one day, I will be blessed to see her again. Until that day comes, I do all I can to continue making her happy. I strive to hear the words, ***"Job well done, thy good and faithful servant,"*** from my Lord.

I no longer spend time seeking acceptance. I remind myself of **WHOSE** I am: *God's daughter.*

Now, don't get me wrong: Life's obstacles still come, but my perspective is completely focused on the hope I now have, the **"JOY"** of where I am headed in life with my children, and knowing I can do **ALL** things through Christ.

Another source of **"JOY"** I have found is being able to encourage others when they allow me a moment to share hope with them to help push forward through some dark times in their lives. Yes, there is a way to find **"JOY"** in those tough situations. I'm grateful trouble doesn't last always, and that **"JOY"** is always there when I seek evidence of its presence! The world didn't give me **"JOY,"** and I **WON'T** allow it to take it away!

Conclusion: God's Joy is for ALL

As you may now see, **"JOY"** means something different to virtually everyone. In *God's Joy Fruit*, however, there is one commonality:

GOD ALWAYS SHOWED UP AND SHOWED OUT!

Through each story penned in this book, I pray that the evidence of God's constant presence was made evident. No matter the trial or tribulation, **HE** never moved; **HE** was always there, protecting and caring for us when we thought we were walking alone. Just the same, He is there for *YOU!*

Please don't think in any way, shape, or form that God doesn't see you and know your heart. We were never promised a life free from pain. It is when we are humbled that we can approach His throne of grace, repent, and ask for forgiveness. God **WILL** make provisions for you to smile again and feel genuine **JOY** deep down in your soul! Allow **JOY** to envelop you today.

Scripture reminds us:
"Until now you have not asked for anything in My name. Ask and you will receive, and your joy will be complete." (John 16:24)

We have not because we ask not—and that also applies to your **JOY**! Get it. Got it? *GOOD!*

The question remains: Considering what you've read, what are you waiting for? Be **JOYFUL**—now!

Compiled by Angela R. Edwards

Tell God ALL about it!

What's *YOUR* **"JOY"** story? What have *YOU* overcome that you thought would keep you bound to the chains of the enemy? Write it down and, if you are so led, share it with others.

BE FREE FROM THAT "THING" TODAY!

_____
_____
_____
_____
_____
_____
_____
_____
_____
_____
_____
_____
_____
_____
_____
_____
_____
_____

God's Joy Fruit

God's Joy Fruit

Compiled by Angela R. Edwards

About the Compiler

Angela R. Edwards is the CEO and Chief Editorial Director of Pearly Gates Publishing, LLC (PGP) and Redemption's Story Publishing, LLC (RSP) — Award-Winning International Christian Book Publishing Houses located in Houston, Texas. In May 2018, PGP was honored as the 2018 Winner of Distinction for Publishing in South Houston, Texas, by the Better Business Bureau (BBB). In 2019, she was awarded BBB Gold Star Certificates for both entities for her exemplary service to the community.

Angela's mantra is *"My Words Have POWER!"* Since its inception in January 2015, PGP has been blessed with an ever-growing and diverse group of almost 100 authors who have penned topics related to faith, love, abuse, bullying, Bible study tools, marriage, and so much more. Their youngest published author was only two years old; their eldest is 75 years old at the time of this publication. To their credit and God's glory, PGP and RSP have collectively over 150 best-selling titles to date.

An affordable publishing option (in comparison to some of the large, traditional publishing houses), PGP and RSP work one-on-one with authors to ensure that financial hardship is not a discouraging part of the publishing process. For those desiring to share their God-inspired messages for the masses, to include both new and 'seasoned' authors, both publishing houses provide unique services and support that many have said "left them feeling as if they are the only author" placed under each company's care.

The Holy Bible states that "God loves a cheerful giver" (2 Corinthians 9:7). To that end, PGP and RSP are frequently found hosting fantastic giveaways. Throughout the past few years, new author contests have awarded authors over $12,000 in services total.

In addition to the aforementioned, Angela is a domestic abuse survivor. Since first telling her abuse-survivor story publicly, she has become a 'Trumpet for Change.' She established the **"Battle-Scar Free Movement"** — an online community of individuals who freely express and share their own overcoming-testimonies. At the same time, they begin the very necessary healing process of the heart, mind, and soul. As part of her God-given mission, she provides abuse victims and survivors a **FREE** opportunity to anonymously share their testimonies in a book series entitled *God Says I am Battle-Scar*

Free. Although the series will be completed in the Spring of 2021, Angela's mission to help individuals heal with the power of their words will continue. Assisting others with the healing process is paramount to her, which propelled her into becoming a volunteer Mentor for the Star of Hope Mission in Houston, Texas.

Angela holds an A.A. Degree in Business Administration from the University of Phoenix and is working towards her B.S. Degree in Psychology with a concentration in Christian Counseling from LeTourneau University. She is a woman of God, wife, mother, grandmother of 12, and trusted friend. Originally a New Jersey native, she has since made Texas her home and embraced the southern culture in all of its fullness. She loves life and affirms daily: **"NOT TODAY, SATAN!"**

Compiled by Angela R. Edwards

Contact the Publisher

Pearly Gates Publishing and Redemption's Story Publishing are always looking for new talent and desires to "birth the writer" in **YOU**! Will *YOU* be next on their list of *Best-Selling Authors*?

Contact us today!

Visit PGP on the Web at www.PearlyGatesPublishing.com

Visit RSP on the Web at www.Redemptions-Story.com

Connect with PGP on Facebook at
www.facebook.com/pearlygatespublishing

Connect with RSP on Facebook at
www.facebook.com/RedemptionsStoryPublishing

Email Angela Edwards, CEO at
pearlygatespublishing@gmail.com

Call 832-994-8797
to schedule your **FREE** 15-minute publishing consultation.

Appendix

Warren, K. (2012). *Choose Joy. Joy is a Conviction.* pp 600. Revell/Baker Publishing Group, Grand Rapids, MI.

Compiled by Angela R. Edwards

www.ingramcontent.com/pod-product-compliance
Lightning Source LLC
Chambersburg PA
CBHW072042110526
44592CB00012B/1520